Intentions – The Silent Architect

Verses Kindler Publication

Verses Kindler Publication.
Website: www.verseskindlerpublication.com

Intentions - The Silent Architect
By: Mr. Khuzema A. Khanwala
ISBN: 978-93-47494-67-3
1st Edition
Price: INR 299/$15

Connect with the author - Intentionbykhuzema.com

Disclaimer

Intentions - The Silent Architect is authored by Khuzema A. Khanwala. The entirety of this published work comprises the original content of the author, who has undertaken diligent efforts in its editing. The characters depicted herein may be fictitious or inspired by real events; however, they are not intended to cause offense or represent any prejudice against any caste or system. Any similarity to the names of actual individuals, locations, or institutions is purely coincidental and serves the narrative. The author bears sole responsibility for the originality of this work; the publisher assumes no liability thereof.

Index

Intentions – The Silent Architect

Author's Gratitude

The reason for writing any book is not that the reader is entirely unfamiliar with the subject. Life, in its many forms and experiences, has already shaped each of us, and much of what is written simply resonates with what we have lived or observed.

In today's era of artificial intelligence, search engines, and the vast expanse of the internet, information is available in endless supply. At the click of a button, one can access knowledge on almost any subject.Even though we have a lot of information available, people rarely spend hours deeply exploring a single topic. Instead, we often look for quick answers or bits of information to meet our immediate needs and then move on, rarely returning to continue our learning.

This is where a book holds its timeless value. Unlike scattered articles or fleeting search results, a book gathers ideas into a coherent, continuous journey. It invites the reader to pause, reflect, and commit to exploring thoughts with depth and consistency, something the fragmented nature of digital browsing seldom allows.

The true importance of a novel or any book lies in its ability to travel with you and be read in your own comfort zone. Whether it is a physical copy you hold in your hands or a digital edition on your device, a book always offers the simple yet powerful tool of continuity. You can pause at any point, mark your place, and return exactly where you left off. In doing so, the rhythm of your reading remains unbroken, and your mind stays anchored within the same stream of thought, instead of being diverted into endless distractions or unrelated topics.

For me, the greatest reward is not fame or praise, but the presence of a reader who begins this journey and stays with it until the final page. If even one person reads this book from beginning to end, that will be my highest achievement and the truest prize I could ever hope to receive.

I would like to express my deepest gratitude to my wife, Arifa, and my daughters, Fatima and Zahabiya, whose constant encouragement gave me the strength to complete this book. Reading has always been my passion, but this work is an attempt to write not only from my mind, but also from my heart and soul.

"And, of course, how can I forget my two little toddlers, Ibrahim & Adam, whose mischievous acts refreshed my mind and kept me smiling with every sentence I wrote in this book."

This journey, however, would not have been possible without the unwavering support of Dr. Kashish Chadha and Radha, who stood by me at every stage, through each line, sentence, paragraph, and finally the last chapter. Their guidance and encouragement ensured that the book did not remain a raw expression but grew into something meaningful and complete.

Time is the most precious resource you possess, more valuable than money or possessions. Each moment is an opportunity that, once lost, can never be reclaimed.

Key Message For Readers

Value every moment and invest it wisely, in growth, relationships, meaningful learning, and actions aligned with your purpose. Managing your time isn't just about being busy; it's about ensuring that your activities bring fulfillment and progress, so you can live without regret and with greater joy.

Your suggestion to seek out and read useful articles is an excellent way to make daily life richer and more meaningful. Keep working on this habit; it will reward you for a lifetime.

I have given examples of different people several times in my book so as to convey my message to the readers to the best of my knowledge.

Chapter 1: Preface – Intention: The Silent Architect

They say time slows down after sixty. Maybe it does. For me, it didn't just slow down, it shifted direction. After decades of working, rushing, problem-solving, and living on life's treadmill, one day I found myself... still. Quiet. The kind of quiet that makes you uncomfortable at first but then invites you to listen more closely, not to the noise outside, but the whispers within me. That's when this book was born.

No, I'm not a renowned author. I've never been on stage giving lectures or receiving writing awards. I'm not even someone who ever thought of writing a book. But I am someone who's lived life, really lived it. I've made mistakes, loved people, misunderstood some, got misunderstood myself, worked hard, faced failure, tasted little victories, and through it all, I've collected stories. Not just events, but emotions. Not just memories, but meaning.

So, why did I start writing at this age? That's a fair question. I guess the simplest answer is: I didn't want to sit idle. Retirement, or rather, slowing down, can be dangerous if you don't use that time wisely. I saw many people around me slipping into hours of television, meaningless scrolling, gossip, or worse, complaining about life. I didn't want to join that club. Not because I thought I was better than them, no, that's not true, but because I believed I had more to give. And still, more to learn.

My days became a blend of household chores, a little cooking here and there, and helping my wife with daily routines, something I must admit I never truly appreciated until I had more time to participate in them. Once the daily tasks were done, instead of wasting time in front of a screen, I opened my laptop and simply... started typing. I didn't plan to write a book. I didn't know what form it would take. But the words came, slowly at first, then faster. Like a dam breaking after years of silent pressure.

What drove this writing was one word: Intention.

I've come to believe that our entire life, every success, every failure, every relationship, every regret, stems from the intention behind our actions. It's that invisible architect shaping our choices. If our intentions are clean, aligned, and pure, life flows better. Even when things go wrong, we feel less regret. But if our intentions are polluted by selfishness, pride, jealousy, or fear, even our victories feel empty. I've seen this too many times to ignore it.

That's why this book isn't about "how to become rich" or "10 steps to success." It's about something far deeper, becoming a good human being. Not a perfect one, just better. The kind of person your inner voice would be proud of. And I truly believe that the ladder to success, real success, starts with becoming a decent human being. That's it. Simple.

But let's pause here. Before you think I'm giving a lecture, let me tell you something very human. I've struggled with the same things you have. I've wrestled with ego. I've had moments of arrogance. I've made decisions with overconfidence and suffered for them later. I've misjudged people. And I've been misjudged too. So, when I speak of these flaws, what I call AEO: Attitude, Ego, and Overconfidence, I speak from experience. Not as a preacher, but as a fellow traveller who has stumbled many times on these rocks.

Let's talk about these three AEOs for a moment.

Attitude is the lens through which we see life. If that lens is cracked, with negativity, bitterness, or self-pity, then even the most beautiful things around us will look distorted. I've seen people who had everything, yet their attitude made them feel poor. And I've met people with very little who carried such grace and gratitude that they looked like kings. Attitude changes your reality more than reality itself ever could.

Ego is tricky. It doesn't shout; it whispers. It makes you believe you're always right. It convinces you that apologizing is a weakness, that compromise is loss, that admitting you're wrong means defeat. But I've learned, often the hard way, that ego doesn't protect your dignity; it damages it. Ego isolates you. It shuts doors, ends friendships, and worse, it deafens you to wisdom.

Then comes Overconfidence. Ah, that bold voice inside that says, "I know it all. I don't need advice." That voice is so convincing, so seductive. It makes you take leaps without checking the ground beneath you. I've fallen flat because of that voice. And every time I had to get up, dust myself off, and say, "I should've listened." Overconfidence isn't a strength. Real strength is being confident enough to say, "I don't know, let me try."

Now, you may ask, what connects all these flaws? The answer again is: Intention.

If your intention is to prove others wrong, to show off, or to dominate, then ego and overconfidence will become your tools. But if your intention is to serve, to grow, to improve yourself, then your attitude will begin to shift. You'll start seeing criticism as feedback, not an insult. You'll see competition as motivation, not a threat. You'll begin to listen more and speak with more meaning. That is the power of pure intention.

I remember one incident that truly made me sit up and rethink the meaning of success. I was at a community gathering, and an elderly gentleman, maybe ten years older than me, was sitting quietly in the corner. Not many people noticed him. No designer clothes, no dramatic entries. But when a little boy tripped and started crying nearby, this man got up immediately, held the boy, checked if he was okay, and gently wiped his tears. No fanfare, just genuine care.

Later, I found out that he was once a senior judge, respected and admired. Yet here he was, completely grounded. That moment stayed with me. I realized, success is not always about wealth, recognition, or status. Sometimes, it's just about how much of your heart is still alive in your daily actions.

This brings me to something I feel deeply about: spirituality. Now, wait. I'm not here to convert you to any religion or debate philosophies. I simply want to say this: all religions, at their core, talk about the same thing, intention. Whether you bow in a temple, kneel in a church, or offer Namaz in The Mosque, none of it matters if your heart isn't in the right place. A man can pray five times a day and still hurt others. Another may not go to a religious place at all, but helps people quietly every day. Who do you think God smiles at more?

I've come to believe: Religion is an intention. And intention is a religion.

The rituals are important, yes. But they are not the end. They are a means to align our hearts with goodness, humility, and service. If, after praying, we step out and gossip, cheat, lie, or harm, then what was the point? On the other hand, if someone steps into the world every day with honesty, courage, and compassion, then even their silence becomes a prayer. This behaviour is better than Prayers.

During the pandemic, I saw many people awaken to this truth. Suddenly, life became uncertain. Fear walked into every home. Rich, poor, educated, illiterate, everyone felt vulnerable. And in that vulnerability, people became more human. They checked on neighbors, shared food, spoke kindly, and remembered God more. But as the world returned to "normal," I saw that kindness faded again. We forgot so quickly. That stillness that taught us so much was replaced once more with the rush of life.

But some lessons, my friend, are worth holding on to.

And so, I write this book not to preach or perform, but to gently remind myself and you that life is not just about running. It's about meaning. And meaning comes when our intentions are aligned with truth, compassion, humility, and awareness.

So, before I move to the next part, I invite you to do something simple.

Pause.
Close your eyes for just ten seconds.
Ask yourself:
What is my intention today?

Not for the whole year. Just today. Is it to be kind? To be patient? To learn something new? To let go of a grudge? To call someone you've ignored? To smile more? To complain less?

Start small. Start now. Because when your intention is in the right place, everything else slowly finds its place too.

Let this be our silent agreement, yours and mine, that before we seek success, fame, or wealth, we will seek clarity of heart.

Because in the end, intention is the silent architect of everything that matters.

The Enemies Within – AEO (Attitude, Ego, Overconfidence)

Let's be honest. We all like to think we're good people.

And for the most part, we are. We don't go around hurting others intentionally, we try to do our best at work, we care for our families, and we help our friends. On the outside, we wear the smile of decency, the robe of responsibility, the face of reason. But peel back a layer, just one, and you'll find something most of us don't like talking about.

Something subtle. Quiet. Dangerous. And internal.

I call it AEO: Attitude, Ego, and Overconfidence. These three are like termites. They don't bring the house down with an explosion. They quietly eat away the foundation until, one fine day, something collapses, and you wonder how it happened. But deep down, you know the truth: it was always there.

So, let's begin with the first one: Attitude.

Now, if there's one thing I've realized over the decades, it's this: attitude is everything. It's the script running behind every reaction, every decision, every relationship.

Let me take you back to my early 30s. I had just been promoted, I had a team of people reporting to me, and for the first time, I had a cabin of my own, complete with glass walls and my nameplate on the door. I felt important. Almost untouchable.

One day, a junior made a mistake in a client presentation. Nothing major, just a misaligned column on an Excel sheet. But I was furious. I called him into my cabin and gave him a public dressing down. His face turned red, his shoulders slumped, and I remember thinking, "Good, he'll be more careful next time."

But that's not what happened. Over the next few weeks, the spark in him vanished. He stopped taking the initiative. He became quiet. Six months later, he left.

Years later, when I met him at another company, he smiled politely, but there was a distance in his eyes. That's when it hit me, my attitude had cost someone their confidence.

You see, it wasn't the mistake that ruined the moment. It was my attitude of superiority. I had let power get to my head. And in doing so, I lost a good team member and a bit of my own integrity.

Attitude is not just about being positive or negative; it's about how we approach people, problems, and possibilities. It shows up in our tone, our WhatsApp, our expressions, and especially in how we treat those who can't offer us anything in return.

A bad attitude doesn't always shout; sometimes, it simply assumes. Assumes we're right. Assumes others are stupid. Assumes people are lazy, incompetent, or beneath us. These assumptions become the lens through which we view the world, and eventually, we see only what our attitude allows us to see.

But attitude can be corrected if we're willing to be honest with ourselves.

Ask yourself this: When someone gives you feedback, do you listen, or do you defend? When you disagree with someone, do you try to understand, ignore them, or do you simply wait for your turn to talk? When someone succeeds, do you feel inspired or threatened?

That's your attitude talking.

Now, let's move to the second enemy: the Ego.

Ah, the ego, it's sly, seductive, and very good at disguising itself.

When I was younger, I used to think ego looked like arrogance. You know, loud voices, chest-thumping, cutting others off. But now I know, ego is much more polished than that.

Ego can look like confidence. It can sound like wisdom. It often wears the mask of self-respect. But in reality, it's that part of us that hates being wrong. It fears looking weak. It resists change. And worst of all, it convinces us that we are better than we actually are.

Let me share a personal failure.

There was a time I was leading a large project. One of my colleagues, younger, sharper, and definitely more up-to-date with technology, suggested a different approach. It was logical, efficient, and well-researched.

But I shot it down.

Why? Not because it was a bad idea, but because it didn't come from me. My ego didn't allow me to accept that someone junior could have a better idea.

And so, we went ahead with my approach. It wasn't a disaster, but it wasn't a success either. When I finally admitted, months later, that his way would've worked better, he just smiled and said, "It's okay, sir." But that moment stayed with me.

It wasn't okay. I had let ego override excellence.

You see, ego makes us want to win every argument, own every room, and prove ourselves, even when no one's asking us to. But ironically, ego is the one thing that keeps us from truly growing.

The ego resists learning. It hates criticism. It demands admiration. And the worst part? It makes us lonely.

Because as the ego grows, empathy shrinks. And when empathy disappears, so do good relationships.

So here's something I've learned: every time you feel defensive, every time you feel the need to prove yourself, pause and ask: "Is it my ego talking... or my truth?" That one pause can save you years of regret.

And now, we arrive at the third and final enemy in this trio: Overconfidence.

Let me say this: confidence is beautiful. It helps you believe in yourself, take risks, chase dreams, and face failure with grace.

But overconfidence?

That's a different beast altogether.

Overconfidence makes you assume success before it happens. It skips preparation. It ignores warnings. It replaces humility with blind faith in your own ability, often leading you straight into trouble.

I remember one particular phase when things were going too well for me. Every project I touched was a hit. My name was being mentioned in the right rooms, clients were praising me, and I started believing I had the Midas touch.

Then came a deal, a big one. Instead of doing my usual diligence, I winged it. I relied on past glory. I trusted my instincts more than the facts.

And I lost the deal.

Worse, I lost credibility. People didn't say anything to my face, but I could feel it, the shift in energy. The pause in their praise.

That's when I realized, overconfidence isn't strength. It's laziness wrapped in self-assurance. It's the refusal to stay a student. And that is a dangerous thing.

In fact, most of the major collapses we see, whether in companies, careers, or relationships, are not because of bad luck. They happen when people stop listening, stop learning, and start believing that nothing can touch them.

Overconfidence blinds us to risk. It underestimates effort. And perhaps most dangerously, it overestimates our importance.

I once read a beautiful line: "Even the tallest mountain is humbled by the sky."

That's how we must be. No matter how high we climb, we must always remember there's a sky above us, of wisdom, of experience, of unknowns. That humility keeps us anchored.

So then, what do we do with these three: attitude, ego, and overconfidence?

We observe them. Not fight them. Because they're not enemies we can kill, they live inside us. They visit us often. But we can learn to recognize them, understand their triggers, and gently show them the door.

The moment you catch yourself saying "I know everything," pause. The moment you snap at someone beneath you in hierarchy, reflect. The moment you find yourself arguing just to win, breathe.

These are the cues. Small ones. But they matter.

The truth is, no one escapes AEO. We all fall prey to them. But those who rise again, wiser, calmer, kinder, gracious, compassionate, are those who take a moment to look within.

I'm not saying I've mastered this. Even today, I find myself struggling. I get irritated, I judge, I assume. But the difference now is, I catch myself faster. I apologize more easily. I listen longer. And slowly, I've seen relationships heal, decisions improve, and peace increase.

Because at the core of it all lies that one word again, intention.

If your intention is to grow, AEO will become your teachers.

If your intention is to dominate, AEO will become your jailers.

It's your choice.

So as we close this part of the chapter, I want to leave you with this thought:

Your biggest opponent in life isn't the market, your competitors, your critics, or your past. It's the three quiet forces within: your attitude, your ego, and your overconfidence. Learn to see them. Listen to them. Then choose to rise above them.

That's how inner leadership begins.

Contentment, Gratitude, and the Power of Quiet Success

Let's talk about something people don't talk about enough anymore: being content.

I know, I know, it's not a sexy word. In a world obsessed with speed, goals, growth hacks, and the next big milestone, "contentment" almost sounds like laziness, doesn't it? Like a word that belongs in your grandparents' vocabulary, not yours.

But here's the thing, I've chased success in its loudest, shiniest forms. I've had moments of fame, positions of power, and even a bank account that made me feel invincible. And yet, the quietest mornings, the ones with no emails, no expectations, no pressure, sipping chai, watching the rain, hearing the birds chirping, those mornings brought me more peace than a thousand standing ovations.

Contentment is not the absence of ambition. It's the presence of alignment, when your actions match your values, when your heart doesn't crave what your soul doesn't need.

It's not about settling. It's about centering.

There was a time when I thought life was a race. Everyone around me was running. Promotions. Houses. Cars. Holidays. The bigger this, the better that. I ran too, because I didn't want to be left behind.

But somewhere along the way, I realized: There is no finish line. Just milestones that keep moving forward.

And then you start wondering, "Am I running because I want to, or because everyone else is?"

That's the moment when the chase starts to feel... empty.

Let me tell you about a friend of mine, Raghav. Sharp man. IIT + IIM pedigree, climbed the ladder at lightning speed, always in the news for some startup, some keynote, some award. He once said something to me over lunch that I'll never forget.

He said, "You know, I spent 20 years proving to the world I was somebody. But now I'm learning how to just be me again."

That's contentment. Not giving up, but letting go of the need to constantly prove yourself.

Gratitude: The Antidote to Noise

If contentment is the calm, then gratitude is the compass.

I wasn't always a grateful man. I took a lot for granted: parents who sacrificed without complaining, a wife who held the home together, a body that worked without needing medicines, a mind that could dream and execute.

But the older I got, the more I saw how fragile it all is.

One accident. One loss. One hospital room, and everything you thought was permanent becomes uncertain.

I remember visiting a government hospital once, volunteering with a friend who worked with cancer patients. I saw a 9-year-old boy smiling while playing Ludo with his mother. Bald head. IV drip attached to his wrist. But his laughter? Pure, bright, like music.

That day, I came home and cried. Not because of what I saw, but because I'd spent so many years complaining about silly things. Traffic. Delayed flights. The AC is not working in a meeting room, need hot coffee all the time.

Meanwhile, a child with cancer could find joy in a board game.

That's when I began my gratitude journal. Stop complaining. In life, you will feel positive energy around you.

Nothing fancy. Just three things every night. Small things. Some days, it's "Had a great cup of filter coffee." Some days, it's "My knee pain didn't flare up today." And some days, it's just "I felt peaceful."

I'm telling you, if you do this for a few months, something inside you shifts. You begin to see what was always there but got buried under comparison and noise.

You start noticing. The kindness in your spouse's eyes. The security of having a home. The way your daughter looks, crawling at you, like you are the universe.

Gratitude is not just a good habit. It's mental wealth. The more you practice it, the richer you feel, regardless of your bank balance.

The Power of Quiet Success

Now, I know what you're thinking.

All this talk about contentment and gratitude is great, but what about ambition? What about achievement?

I hear you.

We've been told that success must be loud. That if it isn't on LinkedIn, it didn't happen. That if people aren't applauding, maybe it wasn't worth it.

But I want to introduce you to a different kind of success. One that doesn't shout. One that doesn't need a spotlight. One that's deeply personal.

Let's call it Quiet Success.

It's the father who chose a stable job over startup dreams so he could be home every night for his kids.

It's the teacher who taught 40 students in a government school and made 38 of them believe they mattered.

It's the woman who walked out of a toxic marriage and rebuilt her life from scratch without bitterness.

It's the man who spent a lifetime taking care of his aging parents and never once asked for credit.

These people may never make headlines. But they live lives that are whole. And in doing so, they become anchors in their communities, examples in their families, and reminders for us all.

Let me share something very personal.

At 60, people often ask me: "What are you most proud of?"

I don't say the awards. Or the promotions. Or the businesses I helped grow.

I say, me & my wife see every day my daughter making video calls showing us our one & half year old grandson making funny actions & trying to stare at us on the mobile screen & gives us a million-dollar smile. My wife still laughs at my jokes. Above all, my childhood friends are still meeting me every weekend.

That's my quiet success.

You see, quiet success doesn't need applause because it's not performed. It's lived. It's not about what you accumulate, it's about what you leave behind in people's hearts.

In a world obsessed with building empires, quiet success focuses on building character.

The Role of Spiritual Alignment

Before we wrap up this part, let's talk about something that often gets left out of "success" conversations: spiritual alignment.

Now wait, don't get nervous. I'm not going to preach. I don't care what your religion is. Or if you even have one.

What I care about, what life has taught me, is that at some point, we all have to ask a big question to ourselves.

Who am I?

What am I doing with my life?

What happens when I die?

These questions visit us quietly, usually in the middle of the night, or in a moment of silence after a long day. And ignoring them doesn't make them go away.

Spiritual alignment doesn't mean chanting mantras or going to the temple every week. It means having a compass inside you, a sense of right and wrong, a connection with something greater than your own self-interest.

It could be God. Nature. Service. The Universe. Consciousness. It doesn't matter what you call it. What matters is that you're not living just for yourself.

Because intention without alignment is like driving a fast car with no idea where you're going.

Some of the happiest people I know have this internal alignment. They may not be wealthy. They may not be famous. But they sleep well. They don't lie. They don't scheme. They give more than they take. And they live with ease.

It took me 50 years to realize that spiritual alignment isn't optional. It's essential.

It doesn't give you all the answers. But it gives you peace with the questions.

The Call to Introspect, Act, and Transform

So here we are. You've walked with me through reflections on intention, the enemies of growth, and the power of quiet success. Now comes the most important part: you.

This book, and this chapter especially, isn't about me. It's about you pausing for a moment and asking:

What is my intention?

In my work, in my relationships, in my personal goals, what is the energy I bring? Is it clarity or confusion? Service or selfishness? Love or ego?

If you're not happy with the answer, that's okay. That's where growth begins.

Take 10 minutes tonight. Sit in silence. Ask yourself what really matters to you. You might be surprised at how much noise you've been carrying.

Then act, not with pressure, but with purpose. Maybe it's a phone call you've been avoiding. An apology you've been postponing. A dream you've buried because you thought it was "too late."

You're not too late. If anything, this is the perfect time.

I started this book at 60 because I realized I still have stories that can serve. I still have wisdom that can flow. And I still have the strength to shift, even if just a little.

So do you.

The next chapters will dive into how intention shapes everything, from relationships to leadership, from crisis to clarity. But none of that will matter if you don't start with this one thing:

An honest look within.

Not to judge. But to understand.

And then, to evolve.

Because at the end of it all, your intentions are your legacy. It's what people feel long after you've spoken. It's what remains when your actions are done.

Let's start there.

Chapter 2 – The AEO Trap: Attitude, Ego & Overconfidence

Cracks in the Foundation – Understanding AEO in Everyday Life

Let me ask you something simple.

Have you ever wondered why some people, despite all their talent, hard work, and even good intentions, don't quite get where they want to be in life? Or why does someone with average intelligence and modest means quietly climb the ladder, one humble step at a time?

It took me years, decades, actually, to realize the answer lies not in external abilities, but in internal barriers. Not the kind of life life throws at us, but the kind we build ourselves.

Three of the biggest culprits? Attitude. Ego. Overconfidence.

I call them AEO, short and sharp, like the impact they leave behind. And if you've ever wondered why your growth feels blocked or your peace disturbed, chances are, one (or all) of these silent saboteurs is playing their part.

So let's break them down, piece by piece, not in the language of psychology, but in the language of life. Middle-class life. The kind most of us live. With EMI bills, water leaks, office deadlines, school reports, and that daily dose of comparison we sip with our morning coffee.

Attitude: The Lens That Colours Everything

Attitude is like a pair of glasses. Once you put it on, it colours the way you want it to be. And if the lens is cracked, distorted, or dirty, you'll blame the world for looking wrong, instead of realizing it's your own vision that needs cleaning.

I'll tell you about Joseph, a colleague I worked with many years ago. Same salary as the rest of us. Same cubicle. Same deadlines. But somehow, he was always grumbling. "Boss doesn't value me." "This company is useless." "What's the point of working so hard?"

He was sharp, no doubt. But that sharpness was dulled by his constant negativity. Any suggestion was met with "This won't work." Any appreciation for others was dismissed with "Favouritism in the department."

Now here's the twist. Just two seats away sat Meena. Single mother. Two kids. Same job, same pressures. But her energy? Completely different. She'd come in, greet everyone, get work done, help others, and leave quietly. When she got promoted, Shyam was furious.

He came to me and said, “Who says, ‘no politics in our company?’”

I said, “Maybe. Or maybe she just didn’t waste time blaming the system and spent that energy improving herself.”

Attitude makes all the difference. It’s the way you show up, not just to work, but to life. A bad attitude creates blind spots. A good one creates bridges.

Ego: The Silent Wall That Blocks Growth

Now let’s talk about the second element of AEO, Ego.

This one’s tricky because ego is very good at wearing a mask. It often pretends to be self-respect. But here’s the difference: Self-respect stands up for yourself. The ego looks down on others.

You may not even realize it, but ego shows up in small, quiet moments.

Like when someone younger corrects you, and instead of listening, you shut down the conversation. Or when your spouse offers advice, and you snap back: “Don’t teach me, I know what I’m doing.” A very good example of the legendary actor Amitabh Bachchan. Despite having such a successful career of 50 years, he said in one of his interviews that his director made him work so hard. He was almost 25 years younger, yet Amitabh accepted it gracefully because there was so much to learn from him.

The ego makes us defensive instead of curious. It makes us protect our image at the cost of connection. And over time, it isolates us.

Think about your own family. Maybe there's an uncle who hasn't spoken to his brother in years because of one argument where neither of them wanted to "bow down." Or a friend who lost a job but won't admit it, walking around pretending everything is fine.

The ego convinces us that admitting a mistake is weakness. But in reality, it's the beginning of wisdom. There is no shame in saying I am still learning, or thanks for contacting me. Usually, we ignore our children, who guide us in our professional life, thinking that we are experienced. That's correct. But aren't ideas and innovations created by younger generations as well? So, keep your ego aside, and if you learn from your children, it's beneficial for you only.

Overconfidence: The Step Before the Fall

Now to the final trap, Overconfidence.

If confidence is a firm handshake, overconfidence is a tight grip that refuses to let go.

It's when we start believing our past success guarantees future wins. When we stop preparing because "I've done this before." When we interrupt people mid-sentence because "I already know what they're going to say."

I've fallen into this trap more times than I'd like to admit.

I remember once being invited to speak at a school function. I'd done so many talks by then that I didn't even prepare. I told myself, "Just go on the stage and everything will fall in place."

Well, I did get on that stage. And I froze in the moment. Not because I didn't have the knowledge, but because I didn't respect the occasion enough to prepare. That overconfidence cost me my rhythm and my respect.

Overconfidence is also dangerous in how it blinds you to risk. You stop listening. You stop learning. You stop growing.

You think only big business owners or politicians fall prey to this? No. Even a middle-class father refusing to adapt to digital banking because "paper passbook was the only good way" is stuck in overconfidence. A student skipping revision because "last time too, he passed in a similar way", that's overconfidence too.

It's not just about big things. It's about everyday decisions where we choose assumption over attention.

How They Work Together (And Trap You Silently)

Now here's the dangerous part: these three don't operate alone.

They feed off each other.

A bad attitude breeds ego. Ego fuels overconfidence. And overconfidence reinforces your negative attitude. It becomes a cycle, and you don't even realize you're trapped.

Let me illustrate.

Imagine a team meeting. You come in thinking no one's as competent as you (attitude). So, you dismiss other ideas (ego). And when your approach doesn't work, you still push it through (overconfidence). When it fails, instead of self-reflecting, you blame others. And the cycle continues.

You don't just lose a project. You lose trust, respect, and time. And most dangerously, you lose the opportunity to grow.

I've seen entire careers go sideways because of AEO. People get stuck in one position for 10–15 years, not because of a lack of skill, but because they are uncoachable. Their managers gave up. Their juniors resented them. Gradually, they became invisible.

Why Middle-Class Lives Are Most Affected

You might wonder, why is this chapter focused so much on middle-class examples?

Because we are the ones who carry the highest expectations with the lowest margin of error. In a simple way, we can say that middle-class people are filling the pockets of rich businessmen. So, why not utilize your potential to be an entrepreneur and join the marathon of big people?

We grow up hearing from our parents, "Study and become something." Our parents didn't have the luxury of mistakes. We often don't either.

So, when we start earning, building a life, inching toward comfort, ego quietly creeps in. "I've made it. I don't need advice."

Or when our cousin buys a car before we do, the attitude shifts. "They're just showing off."

And when we get a little success, overconfidence blooms. "Everything is now easy."

But the middle-class dream is fragile. One mistake, one layoff, one misjudgment, and the progress slips like sand. That's why we can't afford AEO. Neither emotionally nor professionally.

Seeing the Signs

So, how do you know if AEO is becoming a problem in your life?

Ask yourself:

- Do people hesitate to give you feedback?
- Do you often feel misunderstood or underappreciated?
- Do you find yourself thinking, "I'm better than them," more often than you'd like to admit?
- Have you stopped learning new things because you think you already know enough?

If the answer is "yes" to any of these... don't panic. You're not alone. We all fall into these traps. But now that you've seen the cracks, you can begin to fix them.

What Comes Next

This section was meant to hold up a mirror. Not to judge, but to reflect.

In the next section, I'll take you deeper. Into stories where AEO almost broke relationships. Into moments from my own life where I had to swallow pride, admit failure, and rebuild from the inside out.

But before you turn the page, I ask you, just for today, to notice your thoughts.

Watch what your attitude says about others.

Notice where ego tightens your jaw when someone disagrees.

Catch the moment where overconfidence tempts you to ignore preparation.

Just watch. That's the beginning.

Because change doesn't begin with big declarations. It begins with quiet awareness.

And in that awareness lies the power of transformation.

The Inside Job – When the Enemy is You

In Part 1, we explored how Attitude, Ego, and Overconfidence, the infamous AEO, can quietly shape our decisions, derail our growth, and disrupt our relationships. But now, let's go deeper.

You see, there's a moment in everyone's life when you realize the biggest battle you'll ever fight isn't with your boss, your in-laws, or the government, it's with yourself.

Not your enemies.

Not your critics.

But the you inside you, the one that whispers, "You're always right," or "Why should I say sorry?" or "They should know your worth without you saying a word."

That's the moment you realize: sometimes the problem isn't out there, it's right here, sitting quietly in your own chest.

Let me tell you a story. Not of a saint or a great philosopher, but of an ordinary man. Me.

When I Let Ego Run the Show

Years ago, when I was in my late 30s, I was managing a team of about fifteen people in a mid-sized firm. I wasn't the CEO, but within my department, my word was final. I had built a name, someone who delivers results, works late, and doesn't tolerate mediocrity.

At first, I was proud of this image. Who wouldn't be? I had worked hard to earn respect. But over time, that pride grew into something else, an ego.

I stopped listening.

Not in a rude way, I just assumed I knew better. I would sit in meetings and pretend to take feedback. But my mind was already made up before the meeting started.

Then came a day that changed everything.

A young intern, Alex, suggested a change in our client reporting format. He had studied digital design and felt our format was outdated and clunky. My immediate reaction? "Stick to what we've been doing. It's been working well for the past ten years."

He pushed again, very respectfully. "Sir, I just think the clients might appreciate an upgraded version, a more visual layout."

And that's where my ego flared.

I responded, "You've been here three weeks, Alex. Trust me, we know what we're doing."

He nodded silently and sat down. The room was quiet. Nobody spoke.

A month later, we lost a major client to a younger agency. Their feedback? "Their presentation is more advanced, easier to absorb, and more in tune with how we think now."

The truth stung. The same feedback that Alex had tried to offer.

That day, I didn't just lose a client, I lost a chance to grow.

And it made me think, how many other "Alexs" had I dismissed in my life? How many silent warnings had I ignored just because they came from someone younger, less experienced, or simply different?

That's ego. It doesn't shout. It whispers. It protects your pride while quietly poisoning your growth.

Attitude: The Mirror You Avoid Looking Into

Now let's shift gears and talk about attitude.

The dangerous thing about a poor attitude is that it's incredibly sneaky. It often hides behind logic. You'll say things like, "I'm just being realistic," or "I don't expect much, so I won't be disappointed." It feels smart... but it's a trap.

A close friend of mine, Khalid, was sharp. Technically sound. Good at his work. But he carried a chip on his shoulder. He always felt the world was unfair to him, that others with less talent were getting more recognition.

His attitude? Cynical. Defensive. Bitter.

He once told me, "What's the point of trying hard? Everything is about betting. I do my work, take my salary, and go home."

Over time, that bitterness began to affect how he spoke to clients. His responses became dry. His emails, curt. And slowly, his name stopped coming up when promotions were being discussed.

When he got passed over for a raise, he didn't introspect; he blamed the system again. And eventually, he left the company.

Not for a better job, but because he couldn't bear being invisible anymore.

You see, your attitude is not just how you feel. It's how you make others feel. And people remember that more than your degrees or skillset.

Overconfidence: The Foolish Twin of Courage

Of the three AEO traits, overconfidence is the most misunderstood.

Because it looks like strength.

It sounds like "I can handle it." Or "I've done this before." Or worse, "This won't happen to me."

Let me confess something.

When I was in my early 40s, I was offered an opportunity to lead a major new project at our company. It was a big deal, multiple teams, new clients, and tight deadlines.

I should've taken a week to understand the scope, create a team, and plan thoroughly.

But my overconfidence whispered, "You've managed teams before. This will be easy."

So I jumped in headfirst.

Within weeks, things started falling apart. Miscommunication. Missed deadlines. Burnt-out team members. And the worst part? I kept thinking, "This is just a phase, it'll pass."

It didn't. We failed miserably to deliver the project on time. And the fallout was painful; team morale plummeted, client trust dipped, and I had to answer tough questions from top management.

That experience humbled me like nothing else.

Overconfidence is not courage. It's carelessness disguised as confidence. True self-belief always comes with preparation, humility, and a willingness to ask for help.

The Emotional Cost of AEO

Let's move beyond the professional world now.

What does AEO cost you at home?

A friend once told me something profound. He said, "We behave our best with strangers and worst with family."

Think about that.

How often have we shut our spouse down mid-sentence because our ego couldn't handle criticism?

How many times have we assumed we're right in an argument, overconfident that our perspective is the only valid one?

And how often do we let our attitude, our mood, our stress, our frustration, spill onto our kids or parents who had nothing to do with it?

AEO doesn't just ruin our professional lives. It ruins dinner tables. It robs you of moments that matter. Birthdays that end in arguments. Vacations cut short by ego clashes. Silence in the living room because someone wouldn't say "sorry" first.

These wounds don't show up on resumes. But they leave deeper scars.

The Moment of Realization

If there's one gift life gives you when you slow down, it's clarity.

One day, when I was sitting alone in the garden, I asked myself, "Why have some of my closest friendships faded? Why do some people who once admired me now avoid me?"

It was a hard realization to accept: I had let AEO define my personality.

I thought being "strong" meant not apologizing. I thought being "experienced" meant not being questioned. I thought being "confident" meant never admitting I needed help.

But in trying to appear perfect, I had become emotionally distant.

The moment I accepted this truth, something shifted. I reached out to a friend I hadn't spoken to him in 3 years after an argument. I apologized. I didn't justify, I didn't explain, I just said, "I'm sorry for remaining silent."

He replied, "Took you long enough, buddy." And immediately he apologized.

We laughed. We spoke for hours, had tea together, and the next day at Rustom uncle's restaurant. It was more scrumptious than a dinner at a 5-star restaurant.

That's the thing about healing. It begins the moment the ego steps aside and truth walks in.

Resetting the Compass – Tools for Humility and Real Growth

So, we've looked in the mirror, haven't we?

In Part 1, we broke down Attitude, Ego, and Overconfidence, the AEO trio, and saw how they quietly shape, or rather mis-shape, our lives. Now comes the most important part: What do we do about it?

How do we break free from these silent traps?

Well, the truth is, there's no magic formula. No "5 quick fixes to dissolve your ego" kind of nonsense. This is internal work. Quiet work. And it starts with one thing:

A choice.

The choice to see yourself clearly, and then the courage to change gently. Let's walk that road together now.

Step 1: Build Awareness – Catch It As It Happens

The first and most powerful tool? Self-awareness. It sounds simple, but it's often the hardest to master.

We spend so much of our lives reacting. Someone says something, we feel insulted, and our ego kicks in. We're given advice, we feel judged, and our attitude shifts. Something goes wrong, and overconfidence crumbles into self-doubt.

But what if we could catch these moments as they were happening?

Here's something that helped me: Daily Self-Check Prompts.

Ask yourself these three questions every night:

1. Did I interrupt someone today because I thought I knew better?

2. Did I shut someone down because of how they made me feel?

3. Did I listen more than I spoke?

Sounds small, right? But these questions peel off the surface. They show you where your AEO patterns live.

Start journaling. It doesn't have to be fancy. A few honest lines before you sleep. If you're not a writing person, think about it in silence. The point is: awareness begins the shift.

You can't fix what you won't face.

Step 2: Replace "I Know" with "I'm Curious"

One of the most dangerous phrases you can carry in life is: "I already know."

It's a wall that blocks learning. I know because I used to carry it like a badge.

But here's what changed me: I started replacing "I know" with "That's interesting, tell me more."

Try it.

Next time your child tells you about a new app or your junior suggests a better way to file reports, pause your instinct to dismiss. Say, "That's interesting. Walk me through it."

This simple shift does two things:

- It softens your ego.

- And it invites connection.

Curiosity is humility in motion. And believe me, curious people grow faster than confident ones.

Step 3: Listen. Then Really Listen.

There's a huge difference between hearing and listening.

Most of us don't listen to understand. We listen to reply. While someone is talking, we're already crafting our defense. That's ego. That's an attitude. That's fear pretending to be strength.

If you want to reset your compass, practice listening with your whole presence.

Try this exercise for one week:

- When someone speaks to you, don't interrupt.

- Don't reach for your phone.

- Just listen. With your eyes. With your mind. With your heart.

And after they finish, don't jump in with your opinion immediately. Instead, ask, "Can I please suggest?"

Watch how your relationships shift when you become a listener, not a fixer.

Listening is free. But it gives others the most expensive feeling in the world: being valued.

Step 4: Ask for Feedback – And Actually Accept It

Now this one is bold.

Ask someone close to you: "How does my attitude show up to you?"

Or, "Have I ever let my ego come in the way of our connection?"

The first time I asked my daughter this, I'll admit, I was terrified. What if she said something I wasn't ready to hear?

But you know what? She didn't attack. She simply said, "Sometimes, Dad, you give advice before understanding the problem."

That hit me. Because it was true.

The magic lies in what you do next. Don't argue. Don't justify. Just thank them.

That's growth. That's courage.

Step 5: Rebuild from Intention, Not Image

One of the quiet poisons of overconfidence is the obsession with image.

How do I look? What will people say? Will they think I'm weak?

But here's the truth: people remember your intentions, not your image.

Intentions guide your behaviour when nobody's watching. They keep you grounded when compliments rise and criticism stings. If your intention is clear, "I want to grow, not just appear successful", then your ego has no place to hide.

Take a moment today to ask yourself:

- Why do I speak the way I do?
- Why do I lead the way I do?
- Why do I react the way I do?

If your answers come from fear, control, or a need to impress, pause. Rethink.

Real power comes from alignment, not appearance.

Step 6: Introduce Micro-Habits of Humility

You don't need to meditate on a mountain to grow. You just need to practice small acts that break ego and build empathy.

Here are a few:

- Let others go first, whether in conversation or in a queue.
- Say "I don't know" proudly when you really don't know.
- Apologize fast and without a "buy." ("I'm sorry I hurt you" is more powerful than "I'm sorry but I was tired.")
- Celebrate others' success, without attaching your own grades to it. Say "Well done" and mean it.
- Volunteer to help with tasks below your title, mop a floor, carry bags, and serve food at a gathering.

These micro-habits slowly but steadily dismantle pride.

Step 7: Find a Spiritual Anchor – However You Define It

We all need something bigger than ourselves to stay grounded. For some, it's prayer. For others, meditation, nature, music, or service.

I won't dictate a path. But I will say this: a sense of the sacred brings softness. It reminds you that no matter how successful you are, you are still a visitor on this planet.

Whether it's Imam Ali (AS) reminding us that "devotion without understanding is useless," or Lord Krishna advising Arjuna to act without attachment, all spiritual wisdom says the same thing:

Ego blinds. Intention guides.

Start your day with a moment of silence. Not for the world. For yourself.

It could be as simple as:

> "Help me show up today with humility. Help me listen, not dominate. Help me choose kindness over pride."

That 20-second prayer might save you from a 20-year regret.

Step 8: Redefine What Strength Looks Like

We've been taught that strength looks like power, control, and dominance.

But true strength?

It's being kind when you could be cruel.

It's being quiet when you could boast.

It's being honest when lying would be easier.

A friend of mine, who runs a business, once admitted in a team meeting that a recent decision was his mistake. He didn't deflect. He didn't blame.

He said, "I misjudged. I take responsibility."

You could hear a pin drop.

In that moment, his team didn't think less of him. They respected him more. Because strength is vulnerability in action.

What You Gain When You Drop AEO

So far, we've spoken about the costs of AEO. But let me now tell you the gifts you unlock when you release it:

- Clarity: You begin to hear the truth about others and about yourself.

- Peace: You stop fighting unnecessary battles just to prove you're right.

- Connection: Your relationships deepen. People will be attracted to you.

- Growth: You start learning again, like a beginner, curious and open.

- Freedom: You no longer need to impress or compete. You just live.

AEO is heavy. Letting it go will make you lighter.

Closing Thoughts: You Are Not Too Late

If you're reading this and thinking, "I've been like this for years, can I really change?", let me tell you something from experience.

Yes, you can.

Change doesn't require a dramatic life overhaul. It just needs willingness. A little honesty. A little courage. And a lot of grace.

If you shift 1% today, and again tomorrow, imagine where you'll be in a year.

I began this chapter with one word: choice. I'll end it with another intention.

Let your intention be your compass. Not your image. Not your pride. Not your fears.

Every morning, ask yourself:

"What kind of person do I want to be today?"

And then... live that answer, one small action at a time.

Your ladder to peace and purpose doesn't require leaps. Just steps.

Humble, honest, human steps.

And remember, it's never the loudest voice in the room that wins. It's the one who listens, learns, and leads with heart.

That, my friend, is real strength.

And the first step toward true success.

Chapter 3 – Attitude: The Lens of Possibility

The Power of Perspective – Why Attitude Matters

There is a small and oftentimes silent moment that sets the course of your day. Perhaps your tea spills in the morning, or the traffic outside your window is a little too boisterous. Perhaps you answer your phone and read a message that gets under your skin. And in that moment, you have a choice: to respond or to reinterpret.

This decision, as little as it may appear, is where the game of life gets started anew every day.

I didn't always get attitude. Like everyone else, I thought that attitude was just a mood, a temporary mood. A good attitude was to smile when things were good, and a bad attitude was to get short-tempered when things weren't. Easy enough, right? I was mistaken.

But life over a period of time proved this to be not the case. And it is also true that only after going through a great deal of rather challenging and sometimes even painful situations, one realizes that attitude is not a mood but a mindset. It is the spectacles with the help of which we see the world, and the quality of these spectacles is everything when it comes to how clearly everything appears to us.

When I look back on my life at this point, I can trace a pattern. The times I allowed the negatives to settle in, when I indulged in complaining or irritations, nothing positive actually occurred. There were bad experiences that, even when good things happened, I failed to see or acknowledge. And on the other side, when I deliberately decided to keep my chin up, to get out of breath with pain, to do a good thing even when I did not feel like doing anything good, that was a day when I opened the door to progress, peace, and, on rare days, even unexpected joy.

I could not think of a better quote, which perhaps describes the essence of this idea better than any other quote I have heard, attributed to Barack Obama, and goes like this: We are able to create the world of our dreams, as long as we have the strength to start over. That new beginning isn't necessarily out there. It often begins in the mind, in how we decide to perceive a circumstance.

Here's a little story.

Years ago, I was travelling by a local train in Hong Kong between Golden Bell to Grand Nestmouth. The day was hot. The air-conditioner was not working properly, and everybody in the compartment was frenzied, agitated. On the opposite side, there sat one Chinese man, who had kept grumbling away: about the train, about the government, and about the weather, and he even said about his wife! It was a tense atmosphere. But a woman was sitting diagonally opposite us, and she quietly took a book, smiled at her daughter, and began to read her something. A soft story of clouds and waters.

Gradually, the excitement wore away. The grumpy man fell silent. A child in the corner started snickering at the story. Even I felt my attitude ease.

Same train. Same temperature. Same delay.

But two entirely different experiences, created solely by attitude.

That day taught me something I'll never forget: Your attitude doesn't just affect you. It's contagious. It creates ripples. A peaceful heart is able to ease a room. A positive heart can give other people hope to stick on a bit longer.

We are in the habit of attributing our sentiments to the circumstances: I am like this because of work pressure, I am frustrated because events are not going my way. Let's ask ourselves, what would happen if we turn the question around? Suppose that we should put the question as follows: What will happen if I take a different attitude, now?

I do not mean you should play along and act like everything is all right and you are doing fine. On the contrary. There are times in life when things are rough, and it will not help to pretend they are not. However, what will assist is acknowledging that how you approach your challenges is more important than the challenges themselves.

I remember the case of two friends of mine. They were both laid off during the pandemic. One became depressed, blaming the company, the economy, and even himself. He brooded for months, replaying the injustice in his mind.

The other? He spent a week coming to terms with the shock. And then he set about brushing up his skills online. He began to do freelance work, established a network, and in four months had a better income and more freedom than he had ever had. Today, he attributes getting the pink slip to being a blessing in disguise.

What made them different? No qualifications. Not connections. Just attitude.

One saw an end. The other saw a start.

Attitude is strong because it tints your choices. Attitude dictates your responses. Attitude decides if you believe life is a battleground or a playground. If you believe people are challenges or instructors.

I like to say, "Attitude is like the steering wheel of an automobile." You might not be in charge of the traffic, the potholes, or the weather. But you do get to steer. The fact that you get to steer makes all the difference.

We tend to form set attitudes as we become older. "This is just the way I am," we say. But the reality is that attitude is more malleable than we believe. It can be trained, redirected, and honed. And that starts with awareness.

Begin by listening to your inner voice. What are the messages that go through your mind on a normal day? Are they positive or negative? Are they uplifting you or pulling you down? You may be amazed at how frequently your own mind is sabotaging you.

Gratitude, I've discovered, is the seed of a healthy attitude. It doesn't solve problems, but it reframes thinking from what's lacking to what's available. And that reframing leaves room for solutions, patience, even joy.

Another useful tool? Reframing.

Suppose you have a big list of things to do. You can say, "Oh, I have to do all this stuff, my god!" Or you can say, "I am doing this because I have a house, a family, a life." That little change in wording makes a huge difference in energy.

Your words create your world.

The most fascinating aspect? Positive attitude folk aren't individuals with fewer issues. They're individuals who ceased to make issues larger than they are.

I recall meeting a rickshaw driver in Chennai. He had a borrowed cycle, one leg affected with polio, and five members to feed. And yet he wore the biggest smile I'd seen all week. He said, "Sir, I realized he gets to see new people every day. His leg is not working, but his heart is. Why should he waste it on sorrow?"

That man taught me more than any three-month crash course

I want you to take a pause. Ask yourself:

- When was the last time your attitude made a bad situation worse?
- When was the last time your attitude turned a good moment into a great memory?
- Are you steering your day, or letting it steer you?

Keep in mind that we don't look at the world as it is. We look at it the way we want to. And if you change the lens, you change the story.

Bouncing Back – Attitude in Action

If the previous part was the primer for comprehending attitude as a frame of mind, this is the living room, where concepts collide with reality, where words take on flesh. Because it's easy to espouse about attitude, and something else to embody it when the ground's trembling beneath your feet.

Let me begin by sharing with you the story of a fellow I have tremendous respect for.

His name is Joseph, a middle-class man from a humble Mumbai suburb. Just like a blast of wind that extinguishes a well-lit candle, his business went bust overnight. Offices closed. Orders ceased coming. Rent is not being considered by the landlord. His machines fell silent one after the other.

Almost everyone around him panicked or fled quietly from the city. Some grew bitter. Some just gave up.

But Joseph.

He grieved, of course. He felt helpless. But then, one morning, he got up and said to himself, "I may have lost my business, but not my willpower."

He sat down, made a list of his skills, and found something he never knew before: wedding invitation writing and festive occasion cards in Hindi, Marathi, and Urdu had always come naturally to him. During that week, he created a small digital invitation template. He posted it on WhatsApp groups and Facebook. It was crude, plain, but heartfelt.

Within two weeks, he got his first order. And then another. Within three months, he was operating a small-scale, all-digital venture of e-invitations, tapping customers not only in Mumbai but also from other parts of India and Gulf countries.

Same man. Same skills. Different lens. His wife observed that even if Joseph is not showing any pressure on.

Joseph didn't possess money, but he possessed a mindset. That mindset was founded on one strong conviction: "I still have something to give."

That conviction is an attitude in action.

Attitude won't change what happens to you. It will change what happens next.

Samira, a college student, came all the way from Dubai. Smart, optimistic, and full of dreams. But life gave her a curveball early on. She lost her father to an unexpected illness, and her family's financial support structure came crashing down.

Most would empathize if she dropped out. Even she considered it.

But one day her professor observed her pulling away and asked that she stay behind. He just told her, "Your father would be proud of you, whatever. But he'd be proudest if you kept walking. Even when it's tough."

It was the truth that woke something up in her.

Samira began tutoring primary school children in her building for a little money. Just simple math and science. With it, she bought time. She attended school in the mornings, tutored at night, and later graduated first in class.

She now works for a tech firm and pays for her younger brother's studies.in Hyderabad.

That's the ripple effect of attitude.

It starts as a choice, turns into a habit, and becomes a fate. When you help yourself, God will help you.

Individuals ask: "But how do I find my strength when everything is shattering?"

Here's reality: You don't go to find it. You build it. And attitude is your instrument.

Let's take a step back from individuals for a moment and discuss environments. Has anyone noticed how one person's attitude can make or break a team or a household?

If a family is going through a financial crisis. And, the head of the family walks around with a defeated face, talking only about how unlucky they are; that energy spreads like wildfire. But that same person behaves opposite, "We'll tighten our belts, let's not lose our hopes." Immediately, his children and wife will become his superpower, and God will show them the right path.

Attitude creates an atmosphere.

In companies, we frequently discuss "culture." But it is simply the sum of people's attitudes. A single team member who says, "Let's give it a shot," can dissolve a wall of resistance.

I remember a young man named Harry, who worked in a call center. He wasn't the smartest or the most technically skilled, but his attitude was magnificent. Whenever someone had a rough call, he'd pat their back and say, "Tomorrow's another day."

Simple words. Big effect.

When the company was downsizing, guess who they retained?

Not just the top performer. But the top believer. The one who made others believe, too.

Science does too. Research in positive psychology has found that optimists recover more quickly from operations, fare better when subjected to stress, and enjoy stronger, more satisfying relationships.

But we don't need science for that. You and I have felt it.

Consider that one of us in your comments always had a positive thing to say. Whose light she was able to find even in the darkest corner. Perhaps it was your mother or a teacher. Perhaps a friend.

What do you recall about them?

Not what they said.

You recall the way they made you feel.

That's the magic of attitude. It makes an impression.

I want to stop and ask you to reflect here.

Take a moment. Remember being knocked down. A moment when life didn't go according to plan. Perhaps you were rejected, betrayed, or simply let down.

What did you tell yourself at that moment?

Did you say, "I'm cursed, nothing ever works out for me"?

Or did you say, "Okay. This stings. But perhaps this too is part of the path"?

That story, the one you selected, was from your attitude.

And that mindset became your passport or your prison.

I once sat down with an old man at Kensington Gardens, London. He was slowly walking with a cane, greeting each person who passed by. We struck up a conversation, and he shared with me that he had lost his wife two years prior. They had been married for more than 40 years.

I said, "Don't you get lonely?"

He grinned and said, "Yes. But I feel grateful too. Not everyone has 40 years with their soulmate. Some don't even have 4. I miss her every day, but I'm grateful I had her for as long as I did."

That's not merely maturity. That's attitude in its purest form.

He could have been bitter. But he decided to be better.

So, what does attitude in action look like?

It looks like:

- Rising above a defeat.
- Smiling during a storm.
- Inspiring another person, even if your own heart feels heavy.
- Having hope for tomorrow, even when today is tough.
- It's not easy. But it's worth it.

Keep in mind:

Attitude is not pretending that everything is fine.

It's about believing that you have the capacity to deal with it even when it isn't.

Practicing Gratitude – Training Your Attitude Daily

We've spoken about what attitude is. We've walked through the real, emotional terrain of how people have used it to bounce back from unimaginable setbacks. Now comes the most important part of all: how do you build and sustain this kind of attitude, every single day?

Because let's be honest: it's easy to feel positive when life is going well. When everything aligns, when your plans unfold as expected, when your health is good and your people are kind, of course, it's easy to say, "I'm grateful," or "I trust life."

But how do you say the same when things fall apart?

How do you train yourself to choose optimism when the news is grim, the bank account is low, or the people around you are negative?

Building a positive attitude is not about faking happiness. It's not about closing your eyes to pain, or pretending everything is okay when it isn't. That's not an attitude. That's sustaining power.

A strong, grounded attitude is about seeing the truth clearly and still choosing your response mindfully.

That strength comes from practice. And the best practice I know, the most powerful, simple, and universal one, is gratitude.

The Power of Gratitude

I used to think gratitude was just about saying thank you to someone who helped you. A gesture. An act of courtesy. But as I grew older and observed life more deeply, I began to understand something much bigger.

Gratitude isn't just about manners; it's about mindset.

It's about recognizing what you have.

It's about finding light even when there is a shadow.

It's about acknowledging the small blessings that exist despite the chaos.

Science now backs this up. Studies show that people who practice daily gratitude experience better sleep, stronger immunity, lower anxiety, and even longer life spans. But again, you don't need data to feel what you already know.

Think about this: Have you ever had a bad day, and then suddenly remembered something good that made you smile? Maybe a memory, a kind message, or just the sound of rain on your window. That small shift didn't change your circumstances, but it changed your state of mind. That's the power of gratitude.

Let me share a small habit I picked up a few years ago, and which I still practice every morning. Before I look at my phone, I check the news or the messages, I sit quietly and do three things:

1. Five minutes meditation - Say - Oh lord! Thank you for showing me another bright day.
2. 3 times inhale/exhale - Breathing Therapy.
3. 50 push-ups - At the age of 60, it is not easy. But it's not impossible.

It's not always big things. In fact, it's usually not.

These small acknowledgments create a foundation. They ground your mind in appreciation instead of anxiety. They remind you that no matter how chaotic the world is, it is still bright on the other side of the win.

Begin your day, not with depression, but with a good impression.

And a full heart makes better choices.

A man's fate is a fate. Life is just an illusion; don't think too much otherwise, or there will be confusion.

Reframing: The Art of Looking Again

Another powerful tool to train your attitude is reframing.

Reframing is the mental habit of looking at a situation from a different angle.

Let's take a very simple example. You wake up late, you miss the bus or your usual cab, and you're annoyed. It's easy to let that irritation snowball through the day. But reframing might sound like:

"Maybe missing that ride protected me from something I can't see. Maybe this gives me a moment to slow down and breathe."

Let's not forget the latest incident of A.I. flight. Bhoomi Chauhan missed boarding the ill-fated Air India flight 171 by just 10 minutes on 13th June, 2025. Is it true? Maybe, maybe not. But the shift in perspective creates space inside you. It keeps you from spiraling. It opens the door to patience.

You can practice reframing with a simple language tweak:

Change "I have to..." to "I get to..."

- "I have to go to work" becomes "I get to go to work while many still search for jobs."
- "I have to cook" becomes "I get to feed my family."

This isn't a delusion. It's discipline.

It's the choice to tell a better story.

And stories shape lives.

The Attitude Anchor

When you're building a daily habit, you need a cue, something that reminds you to pause, to reflect, to reset.

I call this the Attitude Anchor.

Choose something that already exists in your daily routine. It could be:

- Your morning cup of tea
- A stoplight while driving
- Waiting in a queue
- Ironing your clothes

Use that moment to ask yourself: "Where is my attitude right now?" "Am I resisting or flowing?" "What am I focusing on?"

This one-minute check-in brings awareness. And awareness is the first step to transformation.

I use red traffic lights as my anchor. Instead of getting impatient, I now take a breath and say, "This pause is a gift."

Again, it doesn't change the traffic. It changes me.

Your Ripple Effect

One thing people forget is how much their attitude affects others.

Have you noticed how one grumpy person in a room can ruin the mood? Or how one stranger's smile can lift your day?

Your attitude is not private. It's a broadcast.

Every interaction, every conversation, or a text message carries your energy.

You don't have to be artificially cheerful. But being consciously kind, genuinely open, and thoughtfully optimistic can change not just your life, but the lives around you.

Especially, it reflects a lot in your family.

If you wake up grumbling, your children feel it. If you speak with calmness and faith, even during the struggle, your family learns to trust you.

Leadership begins at home. And it starts with attitude.

One-Day Mindset Challenge

Let me offer you something small, practical, and fun. Try this for one day.

24-Hour No Complaint Challenge

For the next 24 hours:

- Don't complain about anything.

- If something bothers you, ignore it.
- If you slip up, forgive yourself and restart.

End the day by writing three things you learned about your own mindset.

You'll be amazed at how often we complain without realizing. This small challenge brings awareness and shifts your default setting from negativity to curiosity.

You might find yourself saying things like, "Interesting, this didn't go my way. What can I learn from it?"

That question alone can change your entire life.

Practice Over Perfection

Building a positive attitude is like building a muscle. Some days will feel easy. Some days, your old habits will take over. That's okay.

The point is not perfection. The point is practice.

You don't need to change overnight. You just need to begin.

Here's a simple weekly tracker you can use:

Day	Grateful For	Moment, I Reframed	Mood (1-10)
Monday			
Tuesday			
Wednesday			
Thursday			
Friday			
Saturday			
Sunday			

This one chart, filled consistently over a month, can change how you experience life.

Final Thoughts

As we close this chapter, let me leave you with a simple reflection.

Every morning when you wake up, life hands you a paintbrush. The canvas is blank. What you choose to paint is up to you. There will be colors you can't control, unexpected greys, messy spills. But the brush is still in your hands.

Your attitude is that brush.

If you learn to use it well, you can turn even an imperfect day into a meaningful masterpiece.

Let me go back to Barack Obama's quote one last time:

> "We have the power to make the world we seek, but only if we have the courage to make a new beginning."

That new beginning starts not in politics, business, or fate. It starts in your mind. With your attitude.

Choose it well. Nurture it daily. Let it guide your responses, shape your relationships, and build your legacy.

Because ultimately, your attitude is the story your life will tell.

And you, my friend, are the author.

Chapter 4 – Ego: The Invisible Wall

Understanding Ego – The Silent Distorter

Let me begin this part with a quote from Mahatma Gandhi that I've always carried in my heart:

> "The best way to find yourself is to lose yourself in the service of others."

Now pause for a moment and read that again. Gandhi, a man who led millions through a revolution, didn't speak of strength through domination or self-aggrandisement. He spoke of humility, service, and surrender of the ego. That was his way of knowing the self by stepping out of the self.

But isn't that the exact opposite of what the modern world is telling us today?

From the moment we wake up and scroll through our phones, we're being nudged, rather, pushed, toward self-importance. Social media thrives on it. Workplaces subtly reward it. Relationships, too, often suffer under its weight. "Be the best," we're told. "Don't let anyone take you for granted." "Stand up for yourself, no matter what." These aren't wrong in themselves. But when the underlying tone becomes "You must always be right, important, superior," it's no longer about self-respect. It's about ego.

And that's where the distortion begins.

What Is Ego, Really?

We use the word "ego" so lightly. "Oh, he has such an ego," we say, or "Her ego got hurt," as if it's just a personality quirk, a mood, or a fragile piece of glass. But ego is more than that. It's a lens. A quiet filter that overlays every experience, often without us knowing it.

Ego is that little voice that says, "You deserve more than this."
It's the refusal to accept feedback.
It's the swelling pride when someone praises us, and the burning resentment when they don't.
It's the constant comparison, not always out loud, but silently, in the mind.

And worst of all, ego doesn't announce itself. It doesn't tell you it's driving your decisions. It makes you believe that you're acting out of wisdom, confidence, or self-respect.

That's why I call ego the invisible wall.
It doesn't slam into you like a brick; it just slowly rises between you and the world. Between you and growth. You and peace.

Ego vs. Self-Respect: Where Is the Line?

Now here's where most people get confused, and understandably so.

We've been taught to stand up for ourselves, value our worth, and demand dignity. That's self-respect.
But what happens when we start confusing ego with self-respect?

Let me share my own experience with you. Back when I was around 38, I was working in a company that I had helped build from the ground up. I had slogged through weekends, skipped family dinners, and missed countless school functions of my children, all in the name of ambition. I wasn't chasing money; I was chasing recognition. Deep down, I wanted people to say, "He's the pillar here." And they did say it, sometimes.

Then one day, the founder of the company, a man I deeply admired, suggested that we bring in a new business head to restructure operations. I wasn't being demoted. I wasn't losing any pay. But I wasn't going to be the 'go-to' guy anymore.

Something inside me flared up. I said things I shouldn't have. I took it personally. I assumed I wasn't respected. I sulked. I pulled away from team decisions. I told myself, "This is about my self-respect. They can't treat me this way."

Looking back now, I realize that wasn't self-respect.
That was my ego, bruised.

Self-respect would have said: "You've done great work. You're still needed. Let this new person bring fresh value."
Ego said, "How dare they reduce your importance?"
Self-respect would have led to collaboration.
Ego led to withdrawal, coldness, and wasted potential.

The difference is subtle, but vital.

Here's a simple test I use now:
If a reaction is rooted in fear of being small, it's ego.
If it's rooted in awareness of your inherent value, it's self-respect.

One needs constant validation. The other is content even in silence.

How Ego Distorts Heart

You want to know where ego shows up most often? Not in meetings. Not in awards ceremonies. But in the little corners of our relationships.

Have you ever held back from saying "sorry," even when you knew you were wrong?
Ever wait for the other person to text or call first, just to feel powerful?

Ever silently celebrated when someone who criticized you failed?

That's ego. Not love. Not maturity. Not strength. Just ego, playing games to feed its illusion of superiority.

In marriages, I've seen it destroy beautiful bonds. A couple I know, wonderful people individually, couldn't survive because both kept waiting for the other to bend. She thought, "Why should I say it first? He never does." He thought, "I earn, I provide. I deserve the last word." Neither was wrong in their reasons. But ego isn't about logic, it's about fear dressed as pride.

Even in friendships, ego silently whispers: "If they valued you, they'd call more."
And so we let months go by, waiting. Measuring. Silently judging.

But here's what ego doesn't tell you: it's lonely.

Because the ego doesn't want a connection, it wants control.

It's so sneaky, this ego of ours. It wears many masks: intelligence, independence, boldness, when in fact, it's just fear that's scared to admit weakness. Fearful eyes hidden behind dark glasses.

The Ego in Disguise

I remember a moment from a spiritual retreat I attended in Rishikesh. The guru there, a quiet man in his 70s, shared something that hit me like a stone to the chest.

He said, "Even the one who says 'I am humble' must watch himself. Ego sometimes hides in robes of humility, too."

That shook me.

How often do we feel superior, even about being humble?
"I don't need attention like them."
"I'm not showy like others."
Even that is ego, in disguise.

The ego is not always loud. It's not always arrogant.
Sometimes it's the silent inner narrative that constantly judges others. Or secretly believes it's better because it's not like them.

That's why ego is so hard to uproot. It doesn't live on the surface. It hides in our self-talk.

But if there's one thing I've learned over the years, it's this:

The people who truly command respect never demand it.
The people who are truly wise speak least of their wisdom.
And the people who are truly powerful rarely need to prove it.
Their eyes will speak more than their vocal.

Letting Go of Ego: The Gandhi Way

Coming back to Gandhi's quote, "lose yourself in service", I believe that's the most potent medicine for the ego.

Why?

Because when you truly serve, there is no 'I' at the center.
You're not helping someone to look good. You're not being kind to win something back. You're just... present. Open. Empty agenda.

I've seen my own ego melt in moments of service, when I tutored underprivileged kids without expecting praise, when I cleaned up after an event even though I was the supervisor, or when I stood in line with everyone else despite being given a VIP pass.

Each time I let go of the need to feel special, I felt more whole.

There's great irony in ego. The more you feed it, the more you feel insecure.
The more you starve it, the more you feel grounded.

Ego builds tall towers. But peace lives in small huts.

How Ego Affects Marriages, Careers, and Friendships – And How to Stay Grounded

Have you ever been in a heated argument with someone you love and, halfway through, forgotten what the argument was even about? But by then, your voice has gone up a few decibels, your tone is sharp, and all you want is to be right. That moment, my friend, is the ego at play. It's not about solving a problem anymore; it's about winning. And in the process, we lose something far more valuable, the relationship itself.

Let's talk about ego where it hurts the most: our relationships.

Ego in Marriages – The Silent Third Wheel

In many marriages, it's not money or infidelity that breaks the bond first; it's the unspoken tug-of-war of egos. Picture this: A husband feels he deserves respect because he earns, while the wife feels she deserves acknowledgment for running the home. Neither is wrong. But when appreciation isn't expressed, ego fills the gap. Suddenly, gratitude turns into expectation, love becomes transaction, and silence becomes the loudest conversation at the dinner table.

I remember a close friend of mine, Rockey, who was also my neighbour. A kind, hardworking man, married to Anjali, a warm, intelligent woman. But over time, Rocky began expecting a kind of reverence at home that mirrored the respect he got at work. Anjali, meanwhile, wanted equal say in decisions, especially about their kids. Their conversations turned into arguments. Not because their love faded, but because neither could step down from their perceived position of "being right." Years passed. One day, Rocky confided in me, "We still love each other. But we don't like each other anymore."

Ego, my friend, is not always loud. Sometimes, it's quiet resentment. It's the inability to say, "I was wrong" or "You were right." Ego needs validation, but love needs vulnerability.

Ego in Careers – The Roadblock to Growth

In the workplace, ego can be masked as ambition or confidence. But unchecked, it becomes a major hurdle. Ever met a manager who refuses to listen to juniors? Or a colleague who always has to one-up you? That's ego wearing a suit and carrying a laptop.

Let me tell you about Seema, a brilliant marketing professional. In her early years, she was praised for her creativity and drive. But as she climbed the ladder, her openness to feedback shrank. A new intern once suggested a campaign idea that was fantastic, fresh, disruptive, and timely. Seema brushed it off. "What do they know? I've been in this business for 15 years." The campaign launched with Seema's older idea. It tanked. The intern's idea? Later picked up by a competitor, and it went viral.

That's the cost of ego in careers: missed opportunities. Ego stops you from learning, listening, and evolving. The day you think you've arrived is the day you stop growing.

Ego in Friendships – The Quiet Drift

Friendships are supposed to be our safe spaces, our emotional cushions. But even here, ego can create cracks. "Why should I always call first?" "Why did she invite others and not me?" "I'll wait for him to apologize."

My school friend Ashok and I had a fallout over something as trivial as splitting a bill. Silly, right? But neither of us wanted to look like the smaller person. Days turned into months. Finally, one day, I called him just to talk. We didn't even mention the bill. He laughed and said, "Yaar, I was being stupid." I told him, "Me too." That moment healed what the ego tried to destroy.

Friendships drift not because of distance, but because of silence fueled by pride. The ego makes us defensive. It stops us from saying the two things that repair any friendship: "I'm sorry" and "I miss you."

The Root of Ego: Fear and Insecurity

Now let's pause here. Why does the ego even exist? Why do we protect it so fiercely?

Because beneath the ego lies fear. The fear of being seen as weak, wrong, or less than. The fear of being forgotten or not respected. Ego is our shield, our way of saying, "I matter." But the truth is, you already matter. You don't need to shout it from the rooftops or prove it through arguments.

As I aged, I realized something: The most secure people are the humblest. You'll notice it too, the real achievers, the ones who've made it big, are rarely arrogant. They have nothing to prove. Their identity is not tied to approval. That's the paradox: the less you chase validation, the more you earn respect.

Simple Practices to Stay Grounded

So, how do we keep the ego in check? Is it even possible in today's world, where being loud and self-promoting seems to be the norm?

Absolutely. Here are some simple, life-tested tools I've used, and still practice, to keep my own ego on a leash:

1. The Pause Principle

When someone challenges you, especially in a conversation, pause for 3 seconds. Just breathe. Don't respond immediately. In that pause, ask yourself, "Do I want to be right, or do I want to be peaceful?" This one question has saved many of my relationships.

2. Write a Humility Journal

Every night, write down one moment from the day where you were wrong or where someone else taught you something. It could be your child, your driver, or a Waiter. It's a powerful reminder that everyone has something to teach us, if only we listen.

3. Say "Thank You" More Often

Gratitude melts ego. Make it a habit to say thank you to your spouse, your colleagues, and even your house help. Not out of obligation, but out of recognition. You'll notice how your relationships warm up.

4. Seek Feedback, Not Validation

Once a month, ask a friend or colleague: "How can I improve?" Not easy. But if you do it sincerely, your ego will stop treating feedback as an attack and start treating it as a gift.

5. Meditate, Even for 5 Minutes

Ego thrives in chaos. Stillness weakens it. Just sit with yourself, eyes closed, and breathe. Watch your thoughts without judgment. Slowly, you'll notice a space between your thought and your reaction. That space is your ego dissolving.

6. Practice "Being Wrong"

Deliberately let someone else win an argument. Not because you're wrong, but because peace matters more. Watch what happens next. Instead of losing face, you'll earn respect.

Small Steps, Big Changes

These aren't big things. They're not philosophies written on stone. They're just habits. Little, everyday practices that keep the ego from building walls between you and the world.

And remember, this isn't about becoming a saint. We all have an ego. It's natural. But ego should be a shadow, not a spotlight. It should protect, not dominate. The moment it begins to control your actions; it controls your destiny.

Let me leave you with something I remind myself often: Whenever you feel the need to prove something, pause and ask, "To whom? And why?" Most times, you'll realize the only person you need to prove something to... is yourself. And even that can wait till you're calm.

As we move into the next section, we'll explore how ego shows up in the most subtle ways, in our assumptions, in our language, in our inability to truly listen. And we'll discover how dismantling these patterns leads to real liberation.

Because the goal is not to kill the ego. The goal is to live beyond it.

Chapter 5 – Overconfidence: The Optical Illusion

Quotes & Philosophies from Spiritual texts on self–awareness.

Self-awareness is fundamental in the Christian tradition, where scripture encourages examining one's own heart (Proverbs 14:10), speaking truthfully from within (Psalm 15:2), and using God's Word as a mirror to reveal one's true self (James 1:22-25, Hebrews 4:12-13). Cultivating self-awareness is seen as deepening one's relationship both with God and with others, fostering honesty, compassion, and growth toward one's fullest potential.

In the Hindu and Buddhist traditions, self-knowledge or self-awareness is understood as key to spiritual liberation. The Upanishads teach that true knowledge is the realization of the Self (Atman or Conscious) and its unity with the ultimate reality (Brahman), while Buddhist teachings emphasize that self-awareness, profound inner observation, and reflection can liberate the mind from suffering and illusion. Both traditions view self-awareness as a means to transcend limited and mistaken identities, seeing the impermanence of thoughts and experiences.

Classical philosophy, including Plato and Socrates in the West, also emphasized "knowing oneself" as the starting point for wisdom and ethical life. Plato regarded self-consciousness as the soul's recognition of its own nature and its connection to the eternal Forms, while Socratic dialogue was designed to help individuals confront their ignorance, thereby stimulating self-awareness. In the East, Lao Tzu articulated that "Knowing the self is enlightenment," advocating for mastery of the self as the highest form of strength.

Modern philosophy echoed these themes: Descartes' famous "Cogito, ergo sum" encompasses the certainty found in the awareness of one's own existence and thought, an epistemological foundation for all knowledge. Later philosophies, such as Hegel's, further developed the idea that the realization of Spirit (Geist) and freedom unfold through self-consciousness and recognition.

In summary, spiritual texts and philosophies across cultures present self-awareness as a core spiritual discipline, the gateway to deeper wisdom, liberation, compassion, and an authentic relationship with oneself, others, and the divine.

When Certainty Becomes a Trap

It begins subtly. You don't wake up one day and say, "From today, I will be overconfident."

No, overconfidence is far more devious. It clothes itself in competence, swaddles itself in the comforting blanket of your previous successes, and says, "You've got this. You always do." And since you've been correct before, you nod, smile, and believe that voice.

But here's the catch: confidence is necessary. Without it, you'd never go for that promotion, begin that company, or approach someone you look up to and initiate a conversation. The issue arises when confidence blurs over that unseen line and becomes arrogance, when you quit triple-checking your facts, quit listening to criticism, and begin assuming that the world is going to conform to your expectations. That's when the optical illusion sets in. You believe you are climbing uphill towards your aspirations, but in fact, the ground is slowly, subtly sloping downward, and you are being drawn to a gradual decline.

Case Study 1: The Collapse of Nokia – The Colossus That Believed It Could Not Fall

During the early 2000s, Nokia was the crown jewel of the cellular phone business. The brand was ubiquitous, from Indian university canteens to Wall Street executive boardrooms. You essentially owned a piece of virtually unbreakable modern technology if you had a Nokia 3310. Their market share was astronomical, their brand name unparalleled.

But within Nokia's glass skyscrapers, quietly, it was building for a spectacular crash. Executives felt that their supremacy was impregnable. When the iPhone appeared in 2007, most at Nokia dismissed it as a niche luxury item. Touchscreens? Fad. Who would desire a phone without buttons? App stores? A publicity stunt.

That mindset cost them plenty. By 2013, Nokia's cellular business was sold to Microsoft for a fraction of its previous value. The firm hadn't lost market share; it had lost relevance. Their overconfidence wasn't just in their technology but in their assumption that customers would never alter their routines. They confused their current popularity with enduring loyalty, without recalling that the market has no emotions.

The moral? Overconfidence may not always appear as irresponsible expansion or mad choices. At times, it appears as doing nothing, the refusal to change because you think you don't have to.

Case Study 2: The Cautionary Tale of Vijay Mallya

In India, few tales describe the dangers of cockiness better than that of Vijay Mallya. Also known as the "King of Good Times," he established a successful drinks empire and diversified into the high-end game of Formula 1 racing and commercial flying. His airline, Kingfisher Airlines, started with service that was luxury-grade in a market where cheap flying was booming.

At first, Kingfisher was not only an airline but an experience. Red uniformed flight staff, haute cuisine food, celebrity endorsements, it was champagne in the air. But Mallya had underestimated the ruthless economics of the airwaves. Operating a high-end airline in a price-conscious market meant making money to throw away. Rather than rethink the model, Mallya doubled down, believing his brand clout could bend the rules of the game.

What ensued was a fiscal collapse. Kingfisher's losses grew, debt accumulated, and the airline was grounded in 2012. Now, Mallya is a byword for defaults and court cases. His overconfidence, however, was not merely in business; it was also in his assumption that his personal charm and earlier victories could sustain him through an economy regulated by hard figures and narrow margins.

Case Study 3: The 2008 Financial Crisis – When the World's Best and Brightest Missed the Obvious

If overconfidence can bring down companies, it can destabilize economies too. Wall Street's best and brightest thought before 2008 that they had created products so advanced that they had risk-proofed them. Mortgage-backed securities and esoteric derivatives were invincible money-printing machines.

There were warnings, plenty of them, but they were dismissed. After all, the models proved these assets were safe. Even when cracks began to show in the U.S. housing market, the prevailing belief was, "We can't all be wrong." The arrogance wasn't just in the products; it was in the assumption that intelligence equaled infallibility.

When the bubble burst, it created the worst economic crisis since the Great Depression. Folks lost homes, jobs, and savings, not because warning signs weren't obvious, but because the financial elite thought they were too smart to fail.

The Fine Line Between Confidence and Arrogance

It's worth stopping here and saying: confidence is not the villain. In fact, lack of confidence can be as destructive as overconfidence. The true threat is the gradual sliding into exaggerated self-perception from realistic self-assurance.

Imagine confidence as a lighthouse. It illuminates the path, keeps you on track, and helps you make your way through storms without losing it. Arrogance is similar to coating that lighthouse's glass because you believe you don't need it anymore, you'll "just know" the way.

Here are some signs that you may be crossing over that fine line:

Confidence: "I've studied well for this meeting, and I think I can present my argument."

Arrogance: "I'm so competent in this, I don't need to study."

Confidence: "I've achieved success in the past, so I will focus with the same determination on this challenge too."

Arrogance: "My past successes prove I can succeed again, no matter what."

See the difference? Confidence acknowledges the challenge. Arrogance diminishes it.

Why Overconfidence is So Deadly

What makes overconfidence such a lethal trap is that it makes you incapable of diagnosing reality. It is just like having colored glasses-you can see the world, but it is not in its original color. You stop putting questions, checking your blind spot, and stop learning.

The irony? The instant you become complacent about learning is precisely the instant the game is altered. Your competition innovates. The marketplace changes. The rules you believed were carved in granite suddenly disintegrate. You don't see the tumble coming until after you've already fallen.

A Personal Anecdote

I had a young entrepreneur as a client years ago who had started a brilliant, successful food delivery business. His growth statistics in the first year were staggering. Customers adored the app, investors were queued up to invest, and the media couldn't stop writing celebratory profiles.

By year two, rivals had entered the marketplace with lower delivery costs and more efficient logistics. When I told him to reconsider his pricing strategy, he laughed. "We don't compete on price; we're a premium brand." It was a convincing sound, but actually a facade of arrogance was reflected in his reply.

Within months, his order volumes declined. By then, it was too late for him to pivot. The market had already shifted. What hit me most was how preventable the collapse was if only he had not treated early success as a fortress to hold up in, but a foundation upon which to build.

The Illusion of Invincibility

There's an odd psychological bias that sustains overconfidence: the illusion of invincibility. You witness it in athletes who believe they can push their bodies beyond safety limits because they always bounced back before. You witness it in politicians who take more and more risky positions because previous gambles paid off.

The illusion is seductive because it's grounded in actual experience. Prior successes are mighty instructors, but only if you also recall the lessons of prior failures. Excess confidence leads you to believe that failures were simply bad luck and that your inherent genius will save you next time.

Recalibrating Your Confidence

The healthiest professionals, leaders, and people I know continuously recalibrate their confidence. They ask:

Am I deciding this way because the information indicates I should, or simply because I "feel" I'm, correct?

When did I last seek out uncomfortable feedback?

Where I to have to justify this decision to someone I greatly respect, would I be able to do so without waving my hands vaguely?

Such questions don't destroy confidence; they make you stronger. They ground your feet while keeping your head in the air, thinking big.

Overconfidence is the optical illusion that informs you you're ascending when, in reality, you're sliding. It's the desert mirage, you believe you're striding toward water, but it's a reflection of your own hopes. The first step toward never falling prey to it is acknowledging that no one, regardless of talent or experience, is immune.

How Humility Enables Learning and Development

If overconfidence is an optical delusion that makes you perceive yourself larger than life, then humility is the corrective lens that clears vision. Humility isn't thinking less of yourself; it's thinking of yourself less, as famously put by C.S. Lewis. And this nuanced difference is important because most people confuse humility with weakness. In truth, humility is the single biggest driver of learning, adaptation, and long-term success.

Over the years, I've noticed a peculiar pattern in people who remain relevant in their fields for decades: they are the ones who walk into every conversation as a student, not as a senior, experienced person in the room. They can be world champions, billionaires, or spiritual leaders, but their default posture is curiosity, not superiority.

Humility: The Hidden Accelerator of Growth

Consider a dry sponge. It won't take in water unless it has room inside. Once it's full, no amount poured in brings anything new in. Humility operates precisely the same way. When you think that you already know everything, you're like a full sponge, unable to take in new ideas. But when you live with humility, you make room in yourself for fresh knowledge to come in.

The Bhagavad Gita emphasizes the same point in Chapter 4, Verse 34:

"tad viddhi praṇipātena paripraśnena sevayā", "Greet a teacher with respect, question him sincerely, and serve him devotedly; thus you will acquire true wisdom."

The Gita doesn't say "Walk up to the teacher and declare your intelligence." It says bow, inquire, and serve. That sequence matters, bowing lowers your ego, inquiry opens your mind, and service deepens your learning.

This is a principle seen throughout realms. In business, for example, the CEOs who listen most actively to their teams, who avow openly "I don't know" when they don't, are the ones who create the most innovative cultures. Humility in acknowledging ignorance is the beginning of gaining wisdom.

Case Story: The CEO Who Took the Back Seat

A couple of years back, one such tech firm in Bengaluru was facing a downturn. They were being out-innovated by their competitors, and the mood among employees was bleak. Their CEO, Jerome (name changed), was the kind who made decisions swiftly and firmly, qualities that had been very useful during the initial phases of growth. But now, it was the same decisiveness which had turned into complacency. He was not listening to his engineers, pushing aside market research that failed to fit his vision, and paying no heed to the warning signals from the finance division.

All came to a head when one of the flagship product launches tanked. Customers were not impressed, investors were getting restless, and star employees began to quit. Desperate, Jerome went to seek advice from an old mentor, who gave him one plain instruction:

"For the next three months, stop leading from the front. Sit at the back of the room, ask questions, and just listen."

Jerome took this to heart. At meetings, he quit controlling the discussion. He began asking his engineers, "What do you think we should do?" He personally called customers to learn their pain. Gradually, the team felt heard again. New ideas began flowing. In a year's time, the company introduced a new product line that brought back its growth.

Later, Jerome conceded:

"I believed humility would make me appear weak as a CEO. But what it did was make the company strong once again."

This anecdote is a reminder that humility does not slow you down; it resets your direction so you no longer run quickly in the wrong direction.

Why Humility and Learning Are Twins

There is a simple psychological reason humility and learning go together. When you are humble, you naturally:

Ask for feedback rather than avoid it.

Own up to errors immediately, so that you can change direction quickly.

Be curious because you believe there's always something new to discover.

Don't get defensive when questioned, which leaves you receptive to alternative views.

The Dhammapada, a central Buddhist scripture, puts it so well: "One who conquers himself is greater than another who conquers a thousand times a thousand men on the battlefield." Here, "conquering oneself" means subduing the ego, and humility is the cutting sword that slices through its delusions. Once you have your ego under control, learning is pleasure rather than danger.

The Humility of Masters

Now, curiously, some of the greatest masters in any domain are also the humblest ones, not because they have less to show, but because their achievements have taught them just how much more is to be learned.

A.R. Rahman, even after having won Oscars and Grammys, tends to attribute his success to his team, God, and the audience. He once stated, "The more I learn about music, the more I realise how little I know."

In cricket, Sachin Tendulkar had a reputation for bowing his head upon running into the field, a symbolic gesture of respect to the game itself. Though he was referred to as the "God of

Cricket," he played every ball as though it had a right to monopolize his attention, without ever allowing previous centuries to cloud his preparation.

Both Rahman and Tendulkar show us that humility is not the absence of self-worth; it's the recognition that you're part of something bigger than yourself.

Humility in Spiritual Texts: The Consistent Thread

Across spiritual traditions, humility is described as the root of wisdom. In the Bible, Proverbs 11:2 says:

"When pride comes, then comes disgrace, but with humility comes wisdom."

In Sikhism, Guru Nanak Dev Ji again and again stressed nimrata (humility) as a moral virtue that leads you to truth. The Sikh Ardas (prayer) even concludes with the words: "Nanak naam chardi kala, tere bhaane sarbat da bhala", declaring that spiritual progress comes from surrendering to the divine will and desiring good for everyone.

Even the Quran stresses humility in Surah Al-Furqan (25:63):

"The servants of Allah – The Most Merciful are those who walk upon the earth in humility, and when the ignorant address them, they say, Peace."

Walking gently is a metaphor for living without arrogance, a position that permits compassion and understanding to be the dominant emotions.

Practical Ways to Cultivate Humility

Humility may sound wonderful, but being consistently humble is difficult, particularly in cultures that celebrate noisy self-promotion. Here are some simple yet potent practices that can assist:

Daily Reflection on Ignorance

At the end of the day, write down one thing you realized you don't completely get. This little habit keeps you in a learning attitude.

Gratitude Before Sleep

At bedtime, reflect on three individuals who assisted you throughout the day, directly or indirectly. Gratitude helps keep entitlement at bay.

Rotate the Teacher-Student Role
In every team or partnership, deliberately flip. There are times when you lead, and there are times when you learn. Constant change prevents the ego from becoming complacent.

Expose Yourself to Different Worlds
Visit the places where you feel like an outsider. Volunteer in areas you have no idea about. Being the least experienced one in the room is a humbling and growth-filled experience.
The Mirror Test

One of the easiest exercises I have discovered for developing humility is a Sufi teaching. Each morning, after you arise but before you go to work, stand in front of the mirror and ask yourself two questions:

"What do I still need to learn today?"

"Who can I serve without expecting anything in return?"

These questions deflate the ego's hold before it has a chance to balloon in the daytime. The first keeps you open; the second leads you to generosity.

Why Overconfidence Is a Wall, and Humility Is a Bridge

Overconfidence isolates. When we're overconfident, we instinctively send others the message that we don't need their opinion. Eventually, they don't give it. You construct a wall of your own assumptions around yourself.

Humility, in contrast, is a bridge. It opens doors for working together. Others give you more ideas because they feel protected from being judged. You activate collective knowledge rather than just relying on your own.

A 2018 Harvard Business Review leadership study discovered that leaders who scored high on humility were also ranked highest in team performance, innovation, and employee engagement. The research concluded:

"Humility is not a soft virtue; it's a hard driver of results."

A Mahabharata Story

There's a little but striking incident in the Mahabharata in the Rajasuya Yagna of Yudhishthira. While the Pandavas are getting ready to welcome the best guest, everyone recommends Krishna. And yet Krishna, though a king and a warrior himself, personally does the job of washing the guests' feet, serving the meal, and cleaning up afterwards.

When asked, Krishna responds, "Service is not beneath me, because it is through service that love is expressed." This show of humility makes the alliances between the Pandavas so much stronger than any exhibition of power possibly could have.

The lesson learned here is eternal: Power without humility engenders fear; power with humility engenders loyalty.

Closing Thought: Humility Is the Long Game

In a world that is all about "standing out," humility is about "fitting in", not so much in giving up your identity, but in understanding that you are connected to a web of people, opportunities, and experiences.

The Japanese have a philosophy known as Shoshin, or "beginner's mind," which Zen master Shunryu Suzuki defined as: "In the beginner's mind, there are many possibilities, but in the expert's mind, there are few." Humility enables you to maintain that beginner's mind even while your expertise is increasing.

And while overconfidence can have your dreams slope downward without realizing it, humility will cause the slope to incline upward, slowly and steadily, because you're always rising, always learning, always knowing that the mountain has higher peaks before you.

Chapter 6 – Spiritual Teachings Across Faiths: Doing Good Is Universal

When you peel off all the layers of rituals, customs, and dogma, all of the religions are remarkably simple at their core. Doing good, speaking truth, and having pure intentions. These are the recurring themes woven through the great tapestry of the world's faith.

And yet, how soon are we ready to include it? It is easy to find ourselves mired in debates about who is right, whose ritual is superior, or which laws are suited to a good follower. However, setting aside the grandiosity of traditions, it all seems to echo just one eternal truth, which all religions preach: purity in thoughts and goodness in deeds is a mere priority.

There is a lovely saying: Religion is Intention, and Intention is Religion. This in itself could be the summary of spiritual living. You may perform the rituals of prayer, fasting, or flower offering at an altar, but if malice or ego rule your heart, then what is the point of those rituals? However, if you assist someone in distress with selflessness, or forgive when you could have retaliated, then you've accessed the divine on a much deeper level.

Let us tour through various faiths and look at how this central message shows up, again and again, like an underlying harmony in a song.

Islam: Deeds and Intentions

In Islam, there's famous hadith of Prophet Muhammad (peace be upon him): "Actions are but by intention, and every man shall have only that which he intended." This line is a cornerstone of the faith. It tells us that the real measure of our actions is not how they appear externally, but what lies behind them.

Picture someone distributing charity openly with the hidden intention of gaining acclaim. Externally, it appears virtuous, but internally, it is tainted by vanity. Contrast that with a poor fellow who stealthily divides half of his bread with another hungrier than he, and no one is the wiser. Whose act is heavier? Islam would argue the latter, because the motivation was sincere.

There are countless moments like these in everyday life, moments of unobtrusive choices. Refraining from an angry word, opting for truth instead of a workaround, or maybe just smiling at someone, these are little but deep demonstrations of faith. And the remarkable thing is that you don't have to possess grand riches or intellectual wisdom to live this lesson. You simply need a pure heart.

Hinduism: Dharma as Goodness

In Hinduism, the concept of dharma, living in accordance with what is right, is perfectly captured. The Bhagavad Gita stresses that one must work at one's duty without attachment to outcome, but rather with sincerity of action.

Consider the life of Sudama, Krishna's boyhood friend. Sudama was impoverished, yet on visiting Krishna, he brought only a poor gift of puffed rice. He gave it with love, without shame or expectation. Krishna received it gladly, appreciating far more than its value the heart behind the gift.

This tale encapsulates the Hindu perspective: worship and oblation are secondary; what matters is purity of ardor. It also implies that satisfaction with what you possess, and not pursuing boundless wishes, is itself a type of spiritual discipline. When the heart is free from clutter, goodness flows spontaneously.

Christianity: Love Thy Neighbor

Christianity also makes this instruction explicit. Jesus Christ preached love as the most important commandment: The love of the neighbor as to the self. He criticized the Pharisees because they were engaged in specializing in rituals and not in justice, mercy, and faithfulness.

He came up with what is arguably his strongest parable, the parable of the Good Samaritan. A man was left by the road in an injured condition. A priest and a Levite, both religious leaders, traversed them, being far too concerned about ritual purity to stop. A Samaritan, a man who had only collaborated with strangers in the religious elite, interrupted his journey to help and covered up wounds with bandages and ensuring that the man was out of danger.

The moral is ageless: authentic religion has nothing to do with avoiding "impurity" and rituals but with compassion in practice. It is not a matter of how frequently you visit prayer meetings, but how you treat the person standing before you, particularly when it is inconvenient.

Buddhism: Compassion Above All

Buddhism isn't so concerned with a creator god, but it does tell us that the key to a good life is compassion (karuna) and awareness. The Buddha himself discarded strict rituals when they became hollow formalities. He instructed his people to reflect on whether their actions diminished suffering, for themselves and for others.

Consider metta practice, or loving-kindness meditation, where Buddhists wish well to all beings: "May all beings be happy. May all beings be free from suffering." This has nothing to do with burning incense or chanting on autopilot. It's about developing a heart that truly cares.

And this philosophy can be practiced in the most mundane of actions. Letting a stranger through the door, hearing without judgment, or even patience on the road, all become spiritual disciplines when practiced with awareness and compassion.

Jainism: Nonviolence as a Way of Life

In Jainism, ahimsa, or non-violence, is not merely a question of avoiding physical injury but of being kind in thought, word, and action. To criticize somebody, to think unfavorably about them, to use others for one's own profit, all of these are regarded as acts of violence.

A Jain monk once described it like this: "Each time you decide to hold back from anger, you are living nonviolence. Each time you give instead of taking, you are increasing the circle of life."

What's remarkable here is how Jainism reminds us that goodness is not grand action but constant awareness in small decisions. Even sweeping the floor is done with care, so as not to hurt tiny insects. That sensitivity in itself becomes a prayer.

Stories of Everyday Goodness

It's simple to believe that greatness awaits saints or prophets. But quite frequently, the greatest expressions of faith arise from everyday people.

Take the example of a taxi driver who had once left a bag of money in his taxi. Rather than taking it for himself, he went and found the owner and gave back every cent. Why, when asked, would he reply, "If I took it, I'd lose my peace." That is spirituality in action.

Or the store owner who quietly donates free groceries to a struggling family in his community without ever publicizing it. No ceremony, no accolades, simply goodness born of genuineness.

These anecdotes teach us that mundane goodness is much more powerful than performative religiosity. A man who performs goodness habitually, even without calling it "religious," may actually be living the innermost meaning of religion.

Ritual vs. Intention

Now, this doesn't imply rituals are unnecessary. Rituals do matter; they add rhythm to our lives, enable us to slow down, and provide a sense of belonging. Lighting a candle, saying a prayer, or bowing in meditation can all be effective. But the trap is when rituals take center stage, and intentions get lost.

It's the case of polishing the frame of a window and forgetting about the view it provides. The ritual is the frame; the goodness of intention is the view. What's important is that you don't mix the two.

The Role of Contentment

Another string that runs through all religions is the value of contentment. Greed and jealousy, and ego are all children of discontent. But if you can learn to be grateful for what you have, you create room for thanksgiving and generosity.

In Hinduism, santosha is among the niyamas (observances). In Buddhism, it is considered to be freedom from desire. In Christianity, Paul the Apostle wrote, "I have learned to be content whatever the circumstances." And in Islam, the Quran teaches satisfaction with God's provision.

Being content doesn't mean complacency; it means appreciating the present while still striving to grow. It's the soil in which good intentions and good deeds naturally flourish.

Pulling It Together

So, what is it that we learn if we look across Islam, Hinduism, Christianity, Buddhism, and Jainism? That the message of the divine is not concealed in complex rituals or inaccessible teachings. It's in the daily decision to do good, to be generous, to be sincere, and to release selfishness.

The unseen strand between religions declares this: the rituals you do mean less than the heart in which you live.

If you wish to reverence God, serve His creation. If you wish to express devotion, express it through compassion. If you wish to be spiritually wealthy, practice contentment.

Religion should not concern big temples, great mosques, and spectacular churches. Religion is experienced in kitchens, offices, classrooms, bazaars, in the way we talk, share, and serve.

Chapter 7 – Live for a Cause, Not for Applause

Before I begin to discuss this topic, allow me to share a brief personal experience. The book my team and I are writing is not for applause or recognition. It is driven by a greater cause.

Do you see how much we yearn for validation at times more than the activity of actually doing something with purpose? We take a picture of food not because it was delicious, but because people will "like" it. We assist someone, but quietly wait to be thanked. Unconsciously, as humans, we have always wanted to be applauded; it feels great.

The applause, the back-slaps, the rewards; all these flatter our self-image. And the reality of the matter is this: Clapping hands is instant, and popularity fades as quickly as due to a mellow breeze. And what is left is the intention and purpose, and the silent sense of gratification in doing something that counts even when nobody looks.

Happiness, tranquility, rest in bed at night are never measures of the greatest lives or most peaceful of hearts, or the person who has raked in the headlines or the Twitter followers. They were the ones living for a cause, something bigger than themselves. They did not get this ecstatic because they received any form of acceptance, but because they had the inner grinning signal as they had made the correct decision.

Why Inner Fulfillment Trumps External Validation

Let's call a spade a spade, external validation is addictive. It's like sugar: it's a high, but a little while later, you're hankering for more of it. You do something today, and people applaud, but the next day the applause goes away. Then you have to find yourself chasing the next achievement, not for the love of the work, but to hear the applause once more- caught on an endless applause treadmill.

Inner satisfaction, by contrast, is wholesome food. It feeds you deeply, softly, and enduringly. If you make a difference out of sheer intention, assisting a flailing colleague, educating a child without expectation of pay, or planting trees with no hope of accolade, you feel done. No one applauded. No one witnessed. But you know. And that gives your heart a glow.

I recall a teacher saying to me once, "The simplest way to test whether you are living for applause is to ask yourself, would I still do this if nobody found out about it?" If your response is yes, you're living with intention. If your response is no, you're seeking validation.

History is full of examples. Consider Mother Teresa taking the streets of Kolkata, serving the poorest of the poor. She did not set out with a vision of becoming a Nobel Prize winner. She started because her heart could not turn away from agony. Or picture scientists such as Srinivasa Ramanujan, who scribbled math equations on scraps of paper in poverty. He had no idea that one day he would be feted around the globe. What fueled him was not claps but the fire of contribution and curiosity.

"First Deserve, Then Desire" – Meaning in a Middle-Class Life

This ancient proverb, "First deserve, then desire," is a seemingly harsh directive, but contained within lies profound insight. To desire without deserving is to wish for the fruit without sowing the seed. Thousands of middle-class households, from India and everywhere else, have lived by this ethic. They taught their young people not to expect luxury unless they first applied themselves.

Consider a young professional with humble origins. He may fantasize about driving a luxury vehicle, but he first concentrates on developing himself, gaining respect in his field, and saving responsibly. When he finally purchases the car on the day he gets it, the triumph is untainted, not due to envy or competition, but because he earned it through hard work.

Compare this to another man who steals or cheats his way into the same vehicle; the cheers are great, but the inner satisfaction is not there.

This philosophy extends to life itself. If you want respect, first live in such a manner that you will deserve it. If you want love, first become someone who can give it. If you want recognition, first perform work for which recognition is due. Middle-class wisdom is not necessarily going to sound exciting, but because it is genuine, genuineness always prevails over shallow applause.

Individuals Who Did Quite Good Without Credit

There's something deeply beautiful about individuals who do good and walk quietly away. They don't boast. They don't expect praise. Their reward is in the act itself.

I recall hearing about a man from Chennai who used to sponsor school fees for tens of children from his locality. No one knew his identity because he instructed schools to keep it under wraps. When he passed away, his parents realized it was him, and tears freely flowed. That man never found his way into newspapers, but in the hearts of the kids and parents, he was a legend.

In Japan, public schools have janitors who bow to the students each morning, thinking that working for them is an honor. They scrub toilets without expecting publicity. Their silent dignity speaks louder than any words ever can.

Even in mythology, true heroes often perform great acts without boasting. Lord Hanuman, after helping Lord Rama, never demanded a throne, never asked for applause. He saw service itself as the highest joy and reward.

Compare this with today's culture, where every act of kindness is often photographed and uploaded. The spirit of karma is lost the moment it is advertised. Silent good carries far more spiritual weight than loud charity.

In today's world, it is true that some celebrities actively invite paparazzi to their doorstep and even encourage them to shoot videos for social media. This tactic is often part of managing their public image and gaining visibility. However, this behavior has led to criticism, with some comparing such celebrities to "street beggars" who beg for popularity, highlighting how desperate the quest for fame can appear.

The Force of Intentional Service

The Bhagavad Gita again and again makes it clear, nishkama karma: action unattached to outcome. Intention is paramount. Two individuals can do the same thing, let's say, give money, but one does so to actually assist, the other to win praise. Externally, both acts are the same. Internally, they are far apart.

"Religion is intention, and intention is religion." That line captures it all. You may pray for hours, go through rituals with precision, and yet get it all wrong if your heart isn't in the right position. Conversely, one small act of kindness, performed in good faith, has the scent of true spirituality.

Consider a mother preparing dinner. If she prepares it out of love, the dinner feeds more than calories; it feeds the soul. If she prepares it begrudgingly, just out of duty, the food might feed the belly but not the soul. The same with service. It is not the magnitude of what you do, but the motive that generates lasting influence.

And here's the catch: when you quit seeking applause and begin to think in terms of cause, real respect and admiration will usually come as a by-product. Authenticity has a scent. People can smell it. They are attracted to it. Fame sought directly is empty, but fame as a by-product of true service becomes significant.

Being Content in Life Is Very Important

One of the most underappreciated virtues in our world of restlessness is contentment. We learn to hustle, to be constantly reaching for more, to never be satisfied. Ambition is not a bad thing, but when ambition is separated from contentment, it becomes greed. And greed makes sure that no matter how much applause you receive, you're never going to be satisfied.

Contentment is not about laziness or stagnation. It's enjoying what you already possess while working genuinely towards what you aspire to. It's sleeping soundly with thankfulness rather than rolling around with comparison.

I once came across an old man in Varanasi who sold tea on the ghats. He had no platform, no following, and no wealth. But his eyes were shining with tranquility.

When I inquired about his secret, he replied, "Beta, I have enough for today, and I don't care for tomorrow. My happiness is that I get to serve tea to weary pilgrims. What clapping do I require apart from their smile?" That statement was stronger than any sermon.

Contentment is the ground on which real causes take root. When you are content, you are not driven by envy or competition. You are able to give yourself to a cause with an open heart.

Closing Thought

Living for applause is like running after shadows; you pursue them, but they escape. Living for a cause, though, grounds you in something tangible. It might not generate headlines or standing ovations, but it gives you a sort of peace that no crowd can give you.

Therefore, the question that you and I need to ask ourselves is straightforward: what cause am I living for? If no one applauded, would I still be doing what I'm doing? If so, then you are in the right direction. Because applause wears off, but causes endure forever.

Chapter 8 – Integrity in Adversity

The quality of being honest & having strong moral principles, which is not so easy to sustain. It's the peace of mind, the trust you earn, the legacy you leave.

Actual Examples of Ethical Decisions in Challenging Times

There's a basic truth about life that we all find out eventually: it's not in the good times that our character is established, but in the storms. It is easier to do the right thing when everyone is watching; you know there are eyes on you, judgment is coming, and you may get applause or criticism. But what about those idle moments, when there is no one on guard? When the decision is whether to take the shortcut, no one might ever even know about or travel the more difficult path in integrity. That's where integrity is forged.

Integrity has nothing to do with lofty rhetoric or well-planned mission declarations. It is about those invisible decisions, when money is out there in the form of temptation, when authority calls out to tempt you to be bent, when fear tells you, this once, and no one will ever know. But history tells us what men have done when they have stood up, when they have preferred decency to comfort, when they have been willing to prefer principle to gain. Those tales have lived because integrity shines the brightest in the dark.

Let me introduce you to some of these world stories, actual men and women who were tested by circumstances and showed that honesty is not a luxury, but the very core of substantial existence.

Abraham Lincoln – Honesty in Poverty

Whenever honesty is considered in the face of adversity, one name towers above the rest: Abraham Lincoln, who was commonly referred to as "Honest Abe." Long before Lincoln became the President who was to abolish slavery, he was just a poor lad who had to work as a clerk in stores and read the law by candlelight.

There's one well-known story that Lincoln was once a young clerk in a store. He gave a customer a little too much change, only a few pennies less. Most people would have let it pass. Who would ever notice, anyway? But Lincoln took a mile walk home after closing the shop to refund that little sum. To him, every cent counted, not in cash, but in integrity.

Life never gave him ease. His upbringing involved poverty and tragedy, such as the loss of his mother at a young age. But his north star was still integrity. It was that same integrity that later led him to become a leader who was trustworthy. During the most difficult times of the American Civil War, when the country was literally ripping itself apart, Lincoln's integrity was his armor. His foes ridiculed him, his friends questioned him, and pressures urged him to sacrifice. But he never lost his vision of moral freedom and oneness.

Lincoln's biography teaches us that character is not stamped in affluence; it is forged when you possess nothing, and the urge to do the easy thing is greatest. His life teaches us: you can be poor, obscure, struggling, but if you are truthful, you are already rich in character.

Nelson Mandela – Integrity in Prison

While Lincoln's truthfulness was tested in poverty, Nelson Mandela's integrity was tested in the most extreme form of captivity. Locked away for 27 years for opposing apartheid in South Africa, Mandela had ample reason to give up. His captors released him repeatedly if he would only drop his opposition to racial discrimination.

Ponder the cost of that decision: he might have left prison, accepted comfort, and lived in peace. But Mandela didn't do that. Why not? Because his conscience informed him that freedom was not worthwhile if his people were still oppressed. He powerfully declared, "What freedom am I being offered while the organization of the people remains banned?"

Integrity, for Mandela, was never a matter of self-convenience. It was being consistent to justice even in the most excruciating agony. And this is the miracle: when he finally emerged free, rather than letting his bitterness become a wedge, he used his integrity to heal a shattered country. He might have taken vengeance; instead, he decided on reconciliation. That decision, too, was integrity in practice.

Mandela's life shows that even when life takes everything away from you, freedom, family, years, you still possess one power that cannot be taken away: the power of integrity.

Mahatma Gandhi – Truth Over Expedience

Though Indian, Gandhi's message of integrity was global, influencing leaders from Martin Luther King Jr. to Barack Obama. His life was an endless series of tests: prison, beatings, ridicule, and political failures. And yet, his one guiding principle was Satya, truth.

Gandhi believed that shortcuts, even if they seemed effective in the moment, would destroy the dignity of a movement. During India's struggle for independence, many were tempted to meet violence with violence. It was the quicker path, the seemingly effective one. But Gandhi's integrity refused. He declared, "There is no God higher than truth."

Consider the temptation he overcame: in the face of the power of the British Empire, there would have been an easy justification for him to pick up arms. But he took the more difficult route, nonviolence. It wasn't merely a political choice, but an ethical one. It demonstrated that integrity is not about outcomes; it's about the integrity of the path you tread.

And his influence didn't end in India. His integrity rippled across the world, shaping civil rights movements and inspiring generations. Gandhi's lesson? When integrity guides you, even an empire cannot defeat you.

Martin Luther King Jr. – Dignity over Silence

Another man who stretched integrity to the utmost in America was Martin Luther King Jr. This was a world where it would be much safer and easier to have kept quiet. He bravely said, however, that the time is never wrong to do what is right.

The character of King was not only spoken but also acted. He was threatened, arrested, and assassinated. He may have backtracked at every turn, he may have softened his message, decided to take comfort, to avoid confrontation. But somehow, he believed that no amount of dignity can be acquired at the cost of cowardice.

His best examples of integrity were in the Montgomery bus boycott. It was not glamorous; it entailed walking miles instead of riding buses, humiliation, and doing without the comforts of everyday life. Yet King and thousands of others persevered. That boycott was a turning point for the civil rights movement, not because it was easy, but because integrity made it possible.

Malala Yousafzai – Courage at Gunpoint

Integrity is sometimes imagined as a challenge for the leader, the politician, or the great mind. But Malala Yousafzai, a young Pakistani girl, showed that integrity is available to anyone, regardless of age.

Malala desired something basic: education for females. In her part of the world, though, it had been outlawed by extremists. She might have stayed quiet, conformed to the regulations, and stayed safe. Instead, she made her voice heard. She wrote a blog, had interviews, and asserted herself for her right to an education.

The cost? A Taliban shooter boarded her school bus and shot her in the head. She lived, miraculously, and the world believed she would hide in silence. But Malala's integrity was greater than fear. She kept fighting, becoming the youngest Nobel Peace Prize laureate.

Her story shows that integrity isn't about age or status. It's about choosing courage over comfort, truth over silence, even when a gun is pointed at you.

Why Integrity Protects Dignity

Each of these tales has a lesson for us: money, power, shortcuts, they all beckon us. And in the short term, they may even lead us to comfort or acclaim. But over time, they destroy dignity. Integrity is the armor that guard's dignity, even when all else is taken away.

When Lincoln returned the pennies, he was accumulating dignity. When Mandela denied freedom without justice, he safeguarded dignity. When Malala refused to remain silent after being shot, she earned dignity not only for herself but for girls by the millions.

The world tends to gauge success in quantity, wealth, adherents, and votes. But dignity is gauged in silence, in how you rest at night, in whether or not you can look your own eyes in the mirror. And only virtue can uphold that.

Faith, Inner Strength, and the Long-Term Rewards of Ethical Living

What drives a person like Mandela to withstand 27 years in jail without losing his dignity? What lifts Malala from the graveyard after being shot in the head? What sustained Gandhi from fasting and walking miles in the hot sun, eschewing violence despite provocation?

The key is two pillars: inner strength and faith. And the price of maintaining these is not survival alone, but a life full of meaning, respect, and peace.

The Role of Faith in Integrity

Faith is not religion, although religion frequently fosters it. Faith is believing that truth is important, that being good is worth it, even if short-term consequences seem punitive. It is having faith that goodness is not lost, that life, or God, or fate, will ultimately reward it.

Take the case of Dietrich Bonhoeffer, the German clergyman who brazenly defied Adolf Hitler during World War II. He understood the stakes: monitoring, arrest, death. Friends advised him to keep quiet. But faith in God, and in the principle that evil has to be opposed, kept his integrity rooted. Bonhoeffer once said, "The ultimate test of a moral society is the kind of world that it leaves to its children." His belief in that gave him the strength to risk his own safety. He was put to death in a concentration camp, but his integrity left a legacy that still inspires Christians and non-Christians alike.

Faith here was not just about prayer; it was about trusting that truth, even if defeated in the short run, would triumph in the long run.

Or take Rosa Parks, whose refusal to relinquish her bus seat in Montgomery wasn't merely civil disobedience; it was an act of faith. She believed that her dignity as a Black woman counted, that her silent protest would ignite a movement. She afterward testified that her decision was not a product of fear but of faith that God's justice would win out. That act of faith not only transformed her life; it revolutionized the civil rights movement.

Faith gives us that unseen hand that holds us together when temptation is whispering and fear is screaming. It doesn't take away suffering, but it gives suffering a mission.

Inner Strength – The Muscle of Integrity

Whereas belief is the conviction that right will ultimately conquer, inner strength is the muscle that enables you to act on it. It's the spiritual energy that enables you to travel the difficult path when shortcuts are appealing.

Inner strength is typically forged by discipline, self-knowledge, and introspection. It is not constructed in comfort but in tiny, everyday trials. When you stand up to the temptation to embellish on a résumé, when you challenge gossip in the workplace, when you own up to a mistake rather than cover it up, each of these strengthens the muscle of integrity. And when the larger trials come, you're prepared.

Let's consider Winston Churchill during World War II. Britain faced imminent collapse from Nazi bombing. Most politicians called for surrender or negotiation to escape annihilation. Churchill, however, had an inner pillar of strength: his refusal to accept surrender as a viable option, preferable only to death. His speeches, "We shall never surrender", were more than mere rhetoric. They were expressions of an inner pillar that would not compromise. His integrity, supported by that pillar, became Britain's backbone at its worst moment.

Or consider Vaclav Havel, the Czech dramatist who challenged the Soviet government. He might have found safety in quietude, but his inner strength powered his writing and protests. Decades of imprisonment and censorship could not shatter him. Later, he was elected President of a free Czechoslovakia. Havel wrote once, "Keep the company of those who seek the truth, run from those who have found it." His sentiments embodied the humility and strength that constitute inner strength.

Inner strength is not boisterous. It is usually the stillness, patience, or quiet perseverance. But it is this quiet persistence that preserves integrity when all else appears to be broken.

Why Integrity is Harder but Better

One of the wonderful contradictions of existence is that immoral shortcuts tend to appear like the smarter option for the moment. Cheating in an exam will land you in trouble. Telling a lie in a job interview will get you a job. Taking a legal loophole in business will earn your money. At first glance, it appears that it is winning.

But here's the clincher: shortcuts undermine trust, and once you lose trust, it all comes crashing down. Integrity can cost you in the short run, slower promotions, lower profits, and delayed rewards, but over time, it lays a foundation no storm can destroy.

Consider Warren Buffett, one of the wealthiest men in the world. He frequently repeats, "It takes 20 years to build a reputation and five minutes to ruin it.". If you consider that, you'll do things in a different way." Buffett has walked away from sly deals, sidestepped complicated shortcuts, and freely acknowledged errors. Has he missed opportunities due to this? Absolutely. But his long-term integrity has earned him one of the most respected businessmen on earth. Folks invest with him not for fast profits, but because his character has endured decades.

The Long-Term Rewards of Ethical Living

So, what is the payoff of living with integrity? They're not always felt in bank accounts or headlines, but they are profoundly experienced in the inner core of life.

Trust and Respect

Trust is the currency of human relationships. People may admire intelligence or fear power, but they only truly trust integrity. Leaders like Mandela or Gandhi are revered not for their wealth but for their integrity. Even in everyday life, the person everyone turns to in a crisis is rarely the cleverest; it's the one known for honesty.

Peace of Mind

There is a quiet happiness in realizing you need not cover your tracks. No fear of exposure. No worry of being caught lying. Moral living presents you the boon of unperturbed sleep. This serenity cannot be purchased.

Legacy Beyond Life

Fame lasts just a moment, but character begets legacies. Martin Luther King Jr., Mother Teresa, or even business leaders such as Paul Polman (who operated Unilever with an emphasis on sustainability rather than maximizing profit) are not only remembered for what they did, but also for the manner in which they did it.

Inner Growth

With every integrity choice, you build the strength of your willpower. Right living reworks character. After years, it becomes part of your nature. You don't need to "decide" anymore to act right; it is instinct.

Spiritual Writings on Integrity

In all traditions, integrity is celebrated not as something indulgent but as the basis of authentic living.

In the Bible, according to Proverbs 10:9, "Whoever walks in integrity walks securely, but whoever takes crooked paths will be found out." It emphasizes the ultimate security of honesty rather than short-term deception.

The Bhagavad Gita emphasizes unselfish action: "Perform your duty with detachment, without being driven by the fruits of action." This is integrity at its finest, acting honestly, not for accolades or payoff.

In Buddhism, too, the Noble Eightfold Path insists on "Right Action" and "Right Livelihood", evident reminders that spiritual life has no existence except through ethical decisions every day.

The Quran, again and again, brings to the forefront honesty, reminding believers in Surah Al-Isra (17:36), "Do not pursue that of which you have no knowledge. Indeed, the hearing, the sight, and the heart, about all those [one] will be questioned." Integrity here is not a choice, but accountability unto God.

Across the faiths, the message is one: integrity is not convenience but conformity with the timeless truth.

Everyday Heroes of Integrity

While international icons energize us, integrity also sparkles in everyday life. A scientist who won't lie about results. A journalist who turns down a bribe to manipulate a story. An athlete who calls a foul even when the referee didn't see it. These moments don't usually get international headlines, but they cascade quietly, creating cultures of trust.

Take Jesse Owens at the 1936 Berlin Olympics. Competing in Hitler's shadow, Owens not only won four gold medals but also demonstrated integrity in small things. In one of the events, his German rival, Luz Long, gave Owens tips on technique that enabled him to qualify and ultimately win. Owens publicly thanked Long, acclaiming his sportsmanship. Long took a risk of disapproval in Nazi Germany by assisting a Black athlete. Both men exemplified integrity, Owens in accepting assistance, Long in providing it. Their bond became mythical, lasting beyond the cheers of medals.

Integrity in adversity is not sainthood; it's believing that truth counts, and having inner resilience to live by it. The long-term payoff may not always be riches or renown, but it's far more valuable: trust, dignity, peace, and legacy.

The storms of life will arrive, temptations, fears, and tests. Faith provides us with the strength to believe in light during darkness. Inner strength provides us with the will to live that belief. And living ethically ensures that when the storm has passed, we are not merely survivors, we are complete.

Ultimately, applause dissipates, but integrity is the only sound that resounds forever.

Chapter 9 – Ethics in Business & Money: Let Success Follow You

Money is not bad. Let's start there. It is not holy and it is not sinful. It is a tool. A tool that can build hospitals, feed the starving, educate children, and a tool that can pay for wars, tear apart families, or bribe systems into ruin. The difference is not in the money but in the journey taken to obtain it. The journey is what counts.

That is where ethics comes into the picture. Actual success is not determined by how many zeros are in your bank account, but by how clear your conscience is when you retire to bed at night. And as history teaches us, the individuals whose success stood the test of time, and the ones we still look up to, weren't necessarily the ones who earned the most money; they were the ones who refused to do it the wrong way.

Let's discuss why clean money is important, why dirty money never survives, and why ethics and income should grow side by side like roots and branches of the same tree.

Why Clean Money Matters

Take the story of Warren Buffett, one of the world's most respected investors. He is known not just for making money but for insisting on honesty and openness. He often says, "It takes 20 years to build a reputation and five minutes to ruin it."

He built his company, Berkshire Hathaway, on trust. He never invested in businesses he did not understand or in those built on lies. When scandals shook Wall Street, his company survived because its foundation was not only profit, but also honesty.

Now compare that to Bernie Madoff, who also appeared successful for decades. He promised investors guaranteed profits, but it was all fake, the largest Ponzi scheme in history. When the truth came out, families lost their savings, charities collapsed, and Madoff ended his life in prison. He is remembered not for wealth, but for betrayal.

Both men worked in the same financial world. One built clean wealth and respect. The other chased dirty money and ended in disgrace.

The Illusion of Shortcuts

Whenever you take unethical money, in the short term, it seems like a victory. You take shortcuts, you bend a little rule, you grease a few palms, and your company is expanding more rapidly than everyone else. But the illusion wears off.

Consider Enron Corporation in the early 2000s. To the naked eye, it was America's most innovative company. Its managers were hailed as geniuses, its stock was soaring, and employees were proud to sport the Enron badge. Behind the scenes, though, the company was cooking its books, concealing debts, making up profits, fudging numbers.

It lasted for a time. Money flowed in from investors. Executives enjoyed luxuries. But deceptions have a short lifespan. When the scandal exploded, Enron imploded overnight. Thousands of workers lost their jobs, pensions disappeared, and faith in corporate America was undermined for years.

Enron's tale is a bitter reminder: immoral success is constructing a palace on sand. The higher it rises, the more it is destroyed by one wave of truth.

The Peace of Clean Money

There's a saying commonly used in spiritual works: "Contentment is the greatest wealth." Translated into business language, it means that the peace of earning morally is worth much more than the excitement of shortcuts.

Think of a small shop owner who refuses to cheat customers. For example, imagine a grocer who could easily mix water into milk or charge extra for weighing less, but chooses not to. At first, his profits may look smaller than his competitors. But over time, people in the neighborhood trust him. Parents send their children to his store knowing they will not be tricked. His income grows steadily because trust becomes his real capital.

Or take a salaried professional. She files her taxes honestly every year, even when tempted to hide some income. Her colleagues might laugh and say, “Why pay so much when you can get away with less?” But she never has to fear a sudden notice, penalty, or sleepless nights. The peace of mind she earns is far greater than the few extra notes she might have saved by cheating.

Both these examples show the same truth: clean money doesn't hold you back. It builds stronger foundations for growth and gives you the priceless gift of peace.

The Unethical Earnings Cycle and Loss

Dirty money doesn't just blemish bank accounts; it corrodes everything it touches. A fortune built on corruption, fraud, or hidden deals may shine for a moment, but beneath the glitter lies fear. People who earn this way spend more time protecting, hiding, and explaining their wealth than enjoying it.

The truth is simple: unethical gains rise fast, but they collapse even faster. What looks like success today often becomes a downfall tomorrow, leaving behind broken trust and shattered reputations.

On the other hand, honest wealth may grow slowly, but it wears a lasting crown. Clean money carries no fear, no secrets, and no shame. The loop of clean money is slower, but it is steady and it is forever.

The Invisible Currency of Trust

At the center of it all is trust. Clean money fosters trust. And trust is the intangible money that makes wealth grow over generations. Dirty money erodes trust. Once gone, no amount of wealth can purchase it back.

Trust is like oxygen. You don't notice it when it's there, but the moment it's gone, survival becomes impossible. Businesses, too, breathe on trust. Without it, success suffocates.

Everyday Reflection

You don't need to be Warren Buffett to get this. Every professional middle-class individual, every small business owner, makes the same everyday decisions: Do I pad this bill a bit? Do I conceal this income from the taxman? Do I lie on this sale?

It might seem a little inconsequential. But every action builds your reputation, your sanity, and ultimately, your fate.

Because here's the thing: clean money may take longer, but it lets you sleep peacefully. Dirty money may arrive soon, but it steals your peace forever.

And as world history teaches us, the only wealth that's truly worth holding onto is the kind you can openly share with your kids.

Middle-Class Roots, Ethical Fruits

When we talk about ethics in business and money, our minds often rush to billionaires, global corporations, or scandals splashed across international headlines. But if you look closely, the foundation of financial integrity is built in ordinary homes, in small family-run shops, and in middle-class living rooms.

The middle class, often unnoticed, sometimes underestimated, plays a silent yet powerful role in shaping values around money. Their world is not about billion-dollar acquisitions or IPOs; it's about monthly budgets, tuition fees, healthcare bills, and saving up for the family's future. In this world, integrity isn't just philosophy; it's survival.

How Middle-Class Values Shape Financial Integrity

If you grew up in a middle-class family, you probably remember the stories your parents told you:

- "Never take what doesn't belong to you."
- "Even if we don't have much, it should be ours, earned by sweat, not deceit."
- "Better to eat simple food with honesty than feast with shame."

These weren't just moral lessons; they were financial principles.

Middle-class life, with its tight budgets and constant balancing act, naturally breeds discipline. Parents who sit with their children to explain why a certain expense must wait until next month unknowingly pass down something more valuable than money: the value of patience, honesty, and respect for resources.

Lesson 1: Contentment Over Comparison

Middle-class families constantly see wealth around them. A neighbor buys a new car, a relative shifts into a bigger house, or colleagues flaunt luxury vacations. But the middle-class philosophy whispers: "Live within your means." Instead of shortcuts or unethical jumps, they focus on gradual growth, saving a little each month, working hard, and celebrating small wins.

This contentment acts like a shield against greed. And greed, as history shows, is often the root of unethical money.

Lesson 2: Reputation Is Wealth

Ask any small-town shopkeeper what matters most, and they'll tell you: "Hamari izzat hi hamara dhan hai", our reputation is our real wealth. Middle-class people know that in communities, trust is currency. A family name carried with honesty often matters more than a fat bank account.

Think of it: If you need to borrow, whom will you trust? The flashy businessman with questionable dealings, or the humble neighbor who has always kept his word? Integrity creates invisible wealth, trust, respect, and goodwill that money alone can't buy.

Lesson 3: Sacrifice for Principles

Middle-class life is full of tough choices. A father may refuse a bribe at work, even if it means the family struggles a little more that month. A mother may insist on paying full fees rather than using influence to get a concession. These sacrifices teach children that integrity sometimes costs in the short term, but pays richly in dignity and long-term peace.

Stories of Small Businesses with Strong Ethics

Now let's zoom in on the lives of small businesses, the lifeblood of middle-class values in action.

These are not multinational corporations with PR teams polishing their image. They are bakeries, stationery shops, auto repair garages, neighborhood clinics, and local manufacturing units. Their stories rarely make headlines, but they hold timeless lessons about clean money.

1. The Honest Tailor

In a small town in Kerala (India), there was a tailor named Krishnan. He was known for two things: the precision of his stitches and his refusal to overcharge. Customers often told him, "You could easily double your rates; people would still come." Krishnan would smile and say, "If I charge what is fair, people will not just come once, they will come for years."

And they did.

For 40 years, Krishnan stitched clothes for three generations of families. He didn't build mansions or buy luxury cars. But he built something rarer, a name. Today, even though his tiny shop is run by his son, people still say, "Go to Krishnan's tailor shop. They are honest."

That's the quiet power of ethics in small business. It outlives even the owner.

2. The Dairy Farmer Who Refused Adulteration

Milk adulteration is a rampant problem in many parts of the world. Adding water, starch, or chemicals boosts profits but cheats families of nutrition. In Punjab, there was a small dairy farmer named Harjeet Singh who refused to play this game.

When others diluted milk to make money, Harjeet kept his supply pure. Initially, customers complained that his milk was "expensive." But slowly, word spread that his milk was trusted for children and elders. His business grew steadily, because in a market drowning in distrust, one man's ethics became his brand.

Harjeet never needed billboards or advertisements. His brand was honesty, and his customers became his ambassadors.

3. The Stationery That Thrived Through Transparency

STC, a prominent Stationery Wholesale & Retail Company in the Middle East, began its journey with no financial capital, only the strength of hard work, honesty & family unity. Founded by Father & two brothers, the business evolved from small-scale retail purchasing to large-scale imports. Their unwavering commitment to transparency became a cornerstone of their success.

A prime example is their approach to Thermal Labels. While most competitors sell without specifying quantity, STC clearly labels each roll as containing 1000 pieces. This level of honesty, even during challenging early days, earned them the trust of their customers. Today, buyers actively seek out the STC brand, confident in the consistent quality & precise quantity of every product.

4. The Mechanic Who Gave Back Change

We've all heard stories of mechanics overcharging customers by adding "extra repairs." But in a small garage in Manila, a mechanic named Arturo became famous for the opposite. Whenever a job was simpler than expected, he reduced the bill, even when the customer was willing to pay the higher quoted price.

"Why should I take money for work I didn't do?" he would say.

Over time, Arturo's garage became the busiest in the neighborhood. His secret? Honesty was his marketing. His waiting list of customers was proof that clean money multiplies through trust.

Why These Stories Matter

You may wonder: these are just tiny businesses, not billion-dollar corporations. Why do they matter?

Because ethics is not tested only at the top of the ladder. It is tested in every rung we climb. The small shopkeeper who refuses to cheat, the teacher who refuses to take bribes, the clerk who doesn't misuse his position, they are the silent backbone of ethical societies.

If small businesses compromise, corruption becomes a culture. If small businesses hold steady, integrity becomes culture.

Middle-Class vs. The Shortcut Culture

Today, the world is full of temptations. Easy loans, quick profits, online scams, and "get rich quick" schemes bombard us every day. The shortcut culture whispers: Why struggle? Why wait? Just take the fast lane.

But middle-class values resist this. They remind us: "Slow and steady is not weakness, it is wisdom."

Your middle-class parents who saved for years to buy a modest home, who refused shady shortcuts even if it delayed progress, they weren't slow; they were strong. Because now, decades later, that house stands on clean money. No court case, no sleepless night, no hidden skeletons.

The Effect

When a small business runs on ethics, the impact ripples outward:

- Customers learn to trust.
- Employees learn to value honesty.

- Children grow up seeing clean money in action.

Over time, this ripple creates a culture where ethics are normal, not extraordinary. That's why middle-class values matter so much. They don't just shape one family; they shape entire generations.

Everyday Lessons for Us

1. Always choose transparency. Whether you run a tea stall or a tech startup, let your prices, your practices, and your promises be clear.

2. Don't compromise values for temporary gain. That one unethical decision may fetch quick money, but it will stain your long-term brand.

3. Respect small beginnings. You don't need to be a millionaire to run an ethical business. Clean money at any scale has dignity.

Closing Thought

Middle-class life, with all its limitations, hides an incredible power: the power to keep money clean. It teaches us that wealth is not measured in possessions, but in peace. That the pride of handing your children honest money is greater than leaving them a fortune tainted by lies.

The world celebrates billionaires, but maybe the real heroes of ethical business are the nameless tailors, farmers, mechanics, and shopkeepers who keep their word when no one is watching.

Because in the end, success is not about how high you rise, but how clean you stay while rising.

Chapter 10 – No Shortcuts on the Road to Success

Human beings, in every corner of the world, are exposed to the same temptation: shortcuts. Be it business, self-improvement, or even romance, the allure of an immediate payoff glistens like a shortcut on a map--it seems to be faster, easier, and more comfortable. But history and life both continually remind us that short-cuts usually cost a little more in the long run.

One of the most significant reminders of this fact was the pandemic that spread all over the world in 2020. Not only were the health systems and economies tested, but also the character of individuals and institutions in the crisis. It showed who was prepared to bear hardship with patience, discipline, and stamina--and who took a gamble at quick fixes of which the first crash would be fatal.

When we read about world examples of leaders, innovators, and change-makers, one thing is always the same: success, which is long-term, is not brought by shortcuts but hard work, grit, and moral choices.

Pandemic Struggles: A Global Mirror

The COVID-19 pandemic laid bare the vulnerabilities of systems across the world. Companies rushed around, governments lurched from one crisis to another, and people had to face the unknown at a level not experienced for generations. It was a test not just of medical might but of human resolve.

Take New Zealand under Jacinda Ardern's leadership. Whereas leaders for the most part looked for means of reducing effort or downplaying the crisis in order to prevent panic, Ardern adopted an open, hard-grafting, people-first approach. Lockdowns were enforced, messages were unambiguous, and compassion lay at the heart of her message. New Zealand was one of the first nations to successfully flatten the curve. She didn't follow the easy path of denial or half-measures; she took the long, hard path of stringent controls and steady discipline. That path gave her country time, saved lives, and gained worldwide respect.

Other leaders worldwide, on the contrary, cut corners, i.e., denying science, postponing tough decisions, or making economic appearances more important than the lives of people. The result was disastrous: overcrowded hospitals, preventable deaths, and mistrust of the people. What became apparent was the fact that shortcuts in crisis management will always backfire, whereas discipline and hard work will result in sustainable recovery.

The same held true in the business world during the pandemic. Organizations such as Zoom Communications thrived not because they had pursued shortcuts but because they had built years of foundation on dependable technology and scalability. The pandemic merely accelerated adoption. Organisations that spurred ahead into hastily conceived solutions to "cash in" on the crisis tended to fall apart within a few months.

Hard Work vs. Shortcuts: What Effort Teaches

Why is effort more enduring than shortcuts? The reason isn't just results but what the process educates.

Consider Elon Musk. His SpaceX and Tesla odyssey has not been smooth sailing. SpaceX experienced several rocket explosions. Tesla came close to bankruptcy several times. Musk himself acknowledged sleeping on the factory floor, working problems bolt by bolt and circuit by circuit. If Musk had sought shortcuts, cheap outsourcing, corner-cutting in testing, and compromising on safety, the firms would not be the success stories they are now. The very tenacity and perseverance that rode through setbacks eventually became the DNA of their ultimate success.

Compare this with the tale of Elizabeth Holmes and Theranos. Holmes offered a shortcut in medicine: precise blood work in a drop of blood. Investors, politicians, and media were bowled over by the idea. But behind the scenes, the science wasn't ready. Instead of putting in the hard years of research, Holmes and her team faked results and cut corners. For a while, the shortcut looked successful: billions in valuation, magazine covers, speaking events. But truth cannot be shortcut. When the reality emerged, Theranos collapsed, Holmes faced conviction, and the shortcut destroyed not just a company but also trust in healthcare innovation.

Hard work instills resilience, humility, patience, and respect for process. Shortcuts avoid these lessons, leaving one ill-equipped to deal with difficulty when reality catches up.

The Philosophy of Karma and Global Parallels

The Indian philosophy of Karma simply states: "As you sow, so shall you reap." Whatever you seed in the world, effort, intention, or action, will be returned to you. Karma is not mere spiritual verse; it is a worldly principle evident through cultures.

Consider Warren Buffett, one of the richest man in the world. His investment philosophy is based on patience, discipline, and values. Buffett has long maintained that he is not searching for quick profits but for companies with integrity and value for the long term. He avoided shortcuts such as speculative trading or shady business. Now, he is not only rich but respected, uncommon for the same person. His success is karma at work: decades of ethical, hard work coming back as compounding wealth and reputation.

Compare this with the tale of Bernard Madoff, the financier of one of history's greatest Ponzi schemes. Madoff's promise was a shortcut, in essence, guaranteed returns with minimum risk. Thousands believed him. For years, the illusion held. But as is the case with all shortcuts, it finally fell apart. Investors lost billions, lives were destroyed, and Madoff lived out his last years behind bars. The karma of deceit finally got him.

Karma also echoes in the story of Malala Yousafzai. At just 15, she was shot by extremists for demanding girls' education in Pakistan. She could have taken the shortcut of silence to protect her life. Instead, she made the difficult decision to remain an activist, take the risk, and undergo an international level of scrutiny. Her work, bravery, and will became a Nobel Peace Prize and a worldwide education movement. The prize did not come at the beginning, but was profound and lasting.

Why Shortcuts Fail Across Contexts

Shortcuts are appealing because they offer haste. But what they don't consider is sustainability. They can offer immediate gains, but they can't hold up to time, analysis, or hardship.

In politics, shortcuts such as propaganda can win an election but ultimately undermine trust.

In science, shortcuts such as doctored data can gain rapid fame but crumble upon peer review.

Shortcuts in day-to-day life, such as dishonesty in relationships, might provide instant gratification but ultimately culminate in fissures.

Hard work, by contrast, lays foundations that can withstand storms. Nelson Mandela is a powerful illustration. He might have cut corners, taking offers from apartheid leaders to win personal freedom sooner. But he instead took the long path: 27 years in prison. His perseverance and uncompromising moral work provided South Africa with not only a leader but a reconciler and a champion of justice.

The Hidden Rewards of Hard Work

Whereas shortcuts create wealth or celebrity, diligence bestows something much greater: character.

Former Chancellor of Germany Angela Merkel dedicated decades to working quietly, steadily, and without spectacle. She shunned gaudy political shortcuts, opting for discipline, pragmatism, and integrity instead. The outcome? Instead of theatrics, she was given a place among the most highly respected world leaders of her time because of steady, value-based work.

Serena Williams, who is one of the most outstanding sportswomen the world has ever witnessed, did not build a career using shortcuts. The history of the trophy years of hard drills, disappointments, and turn-backs was behind each trophy. The fact that she is able to recover was inspirational to millions, as it demonstrated that not all greatness is about talent; it is about the work to continue regardless of the odds.

Those individuals remind us that the actual reward of hard work is not outside achievement per se, but the internal one that it causes. Hard work will make someone humble, grateful, and kinder to the needy.

The Philosophy of Failures and Letting Go

There's a peculiar way life works: it teaches us more through the bends in the road than through the straight paths. When everything is smooth, when money flows, when applause comes easily, when success seems permanent, we are lulled into thinking we are the authors of control. But when failure strikes, whether through a business collapse, a wrong decision, or simply circumstances outside our command, we are confronted with something deeper: the philosophy of impermanence.

Failures are often painted as full stops, moments where life comes to a grinding halt. But the truth is, they are detours, unexpected turns that reroute us toward lessons we would have otherwise ignored. You've probably experienced this: the interview you didn't clear, the deal that slipped away, the friendship that fell apart. At first, it feels like life slammed the brakes, leaving you stranded. But months, maybe years later, you see the larger picture, that the rejection gave you resilience, the lost deal spared you bigger trouble, the broken friendship allowed you to value loyalty more deeply.

As the philosopher Rumi once said, "Try not to resist life's changes. For change is the hand of God preparing you for greater things."

Failures, then, are not the end of your journey. They are recalibrations.

The Ego and the Illusion of Ownership

When you lose money, whether in business, investments, or through sheer bad luck, there's a burning sensation that almost feels personal. It's not just money slipping away; it's your sense of identity, your sense of control. You feel betrayed, as if life took something that was rightfully yours.

But here lies the trap: was it ever really yours?

Think about it. The wealth we accumulate is always in motion. Today it rests in your bank account, tomorrow it's in someone else's, the day after it circulates into the market, wages, taxes, debts, or gifts. Money never stays. It is not a possession but a temporary companion.

Hindu philosophy beautifully reminds us of this in the concept of Maya, the grand illusion. What we call "ours" is simply entrusted to us for a while. To cling too tightly to it is like holding water in your fist; the tighter you grip, the faster it escapes.

The Bhagavad Gita offers piercing wisdom here. Lord Krishna tells Arjuna: "You have the right to work, but not to the fruits thereof." This single line dismantles the illusion of ownership.

The money you lost was never permanent to begin with. When you start thinking this way, the bitterness of loss transforms into something lighter, acceptance, maybe even gratitude.

A person who loses wealth but still retains inner peace understands this truth: money doesn't belong to us; it passes through us.

Failures as Teachers

If success fills your ego, failure empties it. Both are necessary.

Failures are, in many ways, the real universities of life. They strip you bare, force you to face your vulnerabilities, and compel you to ask questions you otherwise avoid. What did I overlook? What assumptions blinded me? What strength did I underestimate in myself?

Take the story of Thomas Edison. When he failed a thousand times before inventing the light bulb, he didn't see those failed attempts as "dead ends." He famously said, "I have not failed. I've just found a thousand ways that won't work." That perspective, that each failure was a detour teaching him what not to do, was the fuel that eventually led to his triumph.

This is where philosophy turns practical: if we label failures as "dead ends," we end the story too soon. But if we treat them as "detours," we keep walking. And walking long enough is what ultimately brings us to a clearing.

The Philosophy of Letting Go

One of the deepest spiritual practices is the art of letting go. It doesn't mean indifference or laziness. It means refusing to let loss colonize your inner peace.

In Buddhism, the principle of Anicca, impermanence, is at the heart of wisdom. Everything changes: joy, sorrow, wealth, poverty, friendship, solitude. The very nature of existence is flux. To cling to anything, whether success or money, is to invite suffering.

So when you lose money, instead of reacting with despair, try reframing it: "It never belonged to me." This simple mantra shifts the weight from your chest. You begin to see money as energy that flows in and out. And like energy, it will return again, perhaps in new forms, perhaps in ways you never expected.

The Stoic philosopher Epictetus echoed this when he said: "Never say of anything, 'I have lost it,' but 'I have returned it.'" If your child dies, you have to return them. If your fortune vanishes, you have returned it. Nothing is truly yours, so nothing is truly lost. It is simply life reclaiming what it had lent you for a while.

Imagine living with this perspective. Failures no longer break you; they teach you. Losses no longer drown you; they humble you. And through it all, your dignity remains intact.

Money, Satisfaction, and the Middle Path

Here's a paradox we often forget: contentment has nothing to do with how much you have. A billionaire may be restless, while a farmer with two acres may sleep in peace. Why? Because satisfaction is not tied to accumulation but to perspective.

When you start seeing money as temporary, you stop measuring your worth by it. You begin to see life as abundant in other ways, relationships, health, freedom, and time. This is why ancient Indian wisdom places such importance on santosha (contentment). It is not passive resignation but active acceptance, the ability to say, "What I have is enough for now."

Failures and financial losses actually train you in this art. They force you to ask: what really matters? And the answers are rarely about numbers in a bank account. They're about peace of mind, love of family, inner growth, and the quiet joy of integrity.

The Courage of Surrender

Now, let's be clear: saying "it never belonged to me" doesn't mean you stop striving. Life demands effort. Business requires a strategy. Dreams need discipline. What it means is that while you give your best, you loosen your attachment to the result.

There's a powerful story from Zen Buddhism. A farmer lost his horse one day. The neighbors came crying, "Such bad luck!" The farmer calmly said, "Maybe." The next week, the horse returned with three wild horses. The neighbors cheered, "What good luck!" Again, he said, "Maybe." Later, his son broke his leg taming the wild horses. "Such bad luck," the villagers said. "Maybe," the farmer replied. Then a war broke out, and because his son was injured, he wasn't drafted. "Such good luck," they exclaimed. "Maybe," said the farmer.

The point? What we call "failure" or "loss" may be protecting us from something worse. And what we call "success" may bring hidden burdens. The wisdom lies in surrendering the illusion of total control and trusting the flow of events.

Walking Away with Peace

So, what happens when you lose money?

You could fight, cry, complain, or blame. Or you could pause, breathe, and whisper: "It never belonged to me. It passed through me." That acceptance doesn't erase responsibility; you still learn from mistakes, still work smarter, but it keeps your heart light. It keeps you from drowning in bitterness.

Failures, then, become detours, sometimes longer, sometimes more rugged, but always carrying lessons that refine your soul. Money becomes a tool, not a tyrant. And your life becomes less about chasing and more about flowing.

The secret of satisfaction is not winning every time but knowing that whether you win or lose, your worth is untouched. You are not your bank balance, nor your failures, nor even your successes. You are the one who journeys through them, wiser with each detour.

Chapter 11 – Never Underestimate Yourself: Say Yes, I Can

There is a silent enemy that resides within nearly every person.

It doesn't yell. It doesn't burst in. It only whispers, softly, repeatedly, until it's the sole voice you hear.

"You're not ready."
"You're not good enough."
"Someone else would do it better."

That enemy is self-doubt. And more dreams have been killed by it over the years than failure ever could.

Confidence is something the world applauds about yet hardly anybody discusses its fragility. Even the most successful individuals the idols whom we admire have struggled with uncertainty. What mattered to make them stand out among the rest of us is that they never stopped believing in themselves; that is, they did not choose to hear that doubt for an extended period of time.

The Global Epidemic of Comparison

Comparison is now an international game, whether you are in Mumbai, New York, or London.

Social media transformed the lives of everyone into a highlight reel - the dream job, the dream body, the dream family, the dream vacation. You scroll, you compare, and your own reality seems so dull and less.

However, here is the trick, no one is telling about their poor nights without sleep, their rejections, their heartbreaks, their sessions with psychologists. You compare your backstage to the best of some other man.

The truth? Each success story you envy came with a messy, unseen struggle.

Think about Oprah Winfrey, who was let go of her first TV position for being "unfit for TV." Or Walt Disney, who was informed he "lacked imagination." Or Albert Einstein, whose teachers told him he'd "never amount to much."

Each of them heard that voice of doubt within, and the voice of criticism without. Yet they all chose to keep moving.

That's the distinction between individuals who make history and others who meekly surrender: the conviction that their journey, no matter how unsure, is nonetheless worth taking.

The Burden of Expectation

When we are children, we dream with abandon. We dream of being astronauts, musicians, explorers, maybe even magicians. However, there comes a stage in the journey of life when it becomes a checklist of things to do: college, job, marriage, mortgage, retirement.

Your personal and social expectations start to come up like walls between you. You begin gauging your value in achievements - the title, the cash in the bank, the applause.

And when it does not happen - when the promotion does not come about, or the relationship blows right out, you begin to wonder whether you are good enough.

But the reality is just this: You are not your situation. You are what you do with it.

Take J.K. Rowling. Before Harry Potter became a global phenomenon, she was a single mother, broke, and rejected by twelve publishers. Imagine if she had believed those rejections were proof, she wasn't good enough.

Or Steve Jobs, who was fired from the very company he founded. That moment could have destroyed him. Instead, he built Pixar and NeXT, redefining two industries. Years later, he returned to Apple stronger and wiser.

Both Jobs and Rowling shared one thing in common: when life told them "no," they quietly answered, "watch me."

Quotes by Imam Ali (A.S.)

Imam Ali (A.S.), who is famous for his wisdom that transcends time, uttered,

"He who knows himself knows his Lord."

This powerful line assures us that faith in oneself is not arrogance – it's spiritual consciousness. Knowing your own value is to know the divine light that has been bestowed upon you.

He also uttered, “Your disease comes from you, but you do not know it. Your cure is in you, but you do not feel it."

That is, the source of your weakness and the source of your strength are both in you. If you nourish doubt, you become weak. If you nourish faith, you are unconquerable.

Self-belief, therefore, is not merely psychology; it's philosophy. It's a choice every day to pick courage over fear.

The Thin Line between Humility and Self-Doubt

Most people confuse humility with self-deprecation. They believe being humble means remaining small, turning down opportunities, or shying away from praise. But humility has nothing to do with denying your strengths; it's about accepting them without pride.

Nelson Mandela had said,

"I am not a saint, unless you consider a saint to be a sinner who continues trying."

That's humility, being aware of your flaws but still deciding to do what is right.

The antithesis of humility isn't pride, it's fear. Fear that you'll fail, that people will mock you, that you won't be enough. But those fears only have power if you empower them.

Failure as a Detour, Not a Dead End

Winston Churchill famously said,

"Success is not final; failure is not fatal: it is the courage to continue that counts."

Failure doesn't define you; it refines you. It's the world's way of testing how badly you want something.

That attitude, attributing setbacks to steps, is the basis of growth.

So, the next time something doesn't go your way, just remind yourself: this is not the end, it's a redirection.

The Pressure Across Ages

Self-doubt comes disguised in many ways through the phases of life.
In your twenties, it tells you: "You don't know enough."
In your forties, it tells you: "It's too late."
In your sixties, it tells you: "What's the point now?"

But history continues to prove otherwise.

Ray Kroc was 52 when he created McDonald's.
Julia Child was 49 when she published her first cookbook.
Grandma Moses started painting in her seventies.

The timeline is an illusion. Purpose has no use-by date.

It's not about when you begin, it's that you begin.

Breaking the Inner Cage

Self-doubt is like being stuck behind glass. You see the possibilities on the outside, but an unseen force keeps you from reaching them. That "something" is fear, fear of being judged, of being rejected, of failing.

But fear is gone the moment you act.

When Serena Williams came back to tennis during pregnancy complications, the world questioned whether she would ever be the same. But she didn't allow that noise to dictate her story. Her strength encouraged millions of women globally.

Action quiets doubt. Each small action of bravery develops fortitude. Each move toward tells your fear, "You don't own me anymore."

Learning from the Greats

Consider the history of outstanding innovators and leaders; they all started with doubt.

Elon Musk was ridiculed when he declared that he'd make rockets reusable. Jeff Bezos was mocked for offering books online. Malala Yousafzai was advised that girls should remain silent.

If any one of them had paid attention to the world's skepticism, we would have been deprived of some of the most fantastic examples of human courage and conviction.

What they have in common is a simple truth: courage isn't the absence of fear, it's the refusal to let fear dictate.

Philosophy of "Yes, I Can"
"Yes, I can" isn't a slogan; it's a mindset shift.
It's saying yes when situations are screaming no.

It's having faith that your potential isn't based on where you're from, but on where you go.

It entails accepting mistakes as part of mastery.

Barack Obama employed this phrase, "Yes, we can" , not as a political slogan, but as an affirmation of faith in human potential. It rang out with universal appeal because it stated the universal truth: change starts the moment you believe that you can.

Faith and Self-Belief

Belief and faith in oneself are one. Faith is the guide that keeps you grounded when reason fails.

When Mother Teresa passed through the slums of Kolkata with nothing but nothing, she didn't have a clue; she had faith. When

Nelson Mandela spent 27 years in prison, he did not know if there would ever be freedom, but he had a belief.

Faith is believing in the process, even when you cannot yet see the outcome.
It's believing, "This pain has meaning," even if you can't articulate it.

The Universal Lesson

In all philosophies, Stoicism, Buddhism, Sufism, and Christianity, the lesson is the same: Your mind creates your reality.

Marcus Aurelius wrote,

"You have power over your mind, not outside events. Realize this, and you will find strength."

Buddha said,

"The mind is everything. What you think, you become."

Various religions, same message, the quality of your thinking determines the quality of your life.

And when you say, "I can't," you are designing a life where you won't. And when you say, "I can," even if you're not sure, you create a door that opens to new possibilities.

In the End

You are better than you know. The issue isn't that the world doesn't think much of you; it's that you hear them and believe them.

The moment you cease doubting your value is the moment your life will transform.

Because when you finally start believing in yourself, really, sincerely, the world is left with no other option but to believe in you too.

So the next time the little voice of doubt comes creeping in, tell it softly but firmly:

"Yes, I can."

Chapter 12 – Forgiveness & The Intention to Heal

Forgiveness is one of those ideals that everyone discusses but very few really comprehend. It's confused with weakness, with letting someone "off the hook," or with pretending that what occurred did not happen. But authentic forgiveness has absolutely nothing to do with the other person; it has everything to do with releasing yourself. It has to do with leaving a cage that you didn't even know you constructed with your own anger. Forgiveness has been called the pathway between suffering and peace across cultures, religions, and history. The wish to heal is actually the desire.

We shall begin with a general fact: anger is heavy. The longer you wear it, the more it twists your spine and blurs your heart. The most famous definition of forgiveness is that of Nelson Mandela, who at one time stated: I am sipping poison and I hope it kills my enemies. He was not avenging anything when he walked out of Robben Island, having spent the last 27 years behind prison bars. He had vision. Mandela could have chosen to seek revenge, but he chose to seek unity. His forgiveness was not simple, but political, biblical, and liberating. It was the basis on which South Africa started to mend.

The Power of Letting Go

By being bitter, we are literally in the past. When we remember the scene of betrayal or rejection or injustice, we are opening a festering wound. Forgiveness does not concern forgetting. It is of recalling wisely and not painfully.

Take the case of Desmond Tutu, who was the chairman of the South African Truth and Reconciliation Commission after apartheid. It was a radical process; it needed victims and offenders to speak their truths, to hear, and to forgive. It was not easy; there were tears, there were tantrums, and there was deep silence in the atmosphere. But that universal exercise of forgiveness was a national psychotherapy. Tutu used to say, "Without forgiveness, there is no future." Those are not words about a nation; they are words about every human heart that has ever suffered.

Forgiveness is not a one-time process. It begins with the resolution to forgive, although you may not be ready yet. You do not need to feel so immediately; you simply need to decide to desire peace more than pain.

Forgiving Yourself: The Hardest Step

It is easier for us to forgive others but not ourselves. We continue to beat ourselves up over past sins, lost love, or miscalculations. Guilt doesn't make you noble; it makes you stuck.

How can we forget Oprah Winfrey's story? She was born into poverty, abused, and told she would never succeed. She bore shame for many years. But when she started talking freely about her suffering, she not only recovered herself but also enabled millions of people to recover as well. Oprah frequently says, "Forgiveness is giving up the hope that the past could have been any different." That one sentence reroutes the attention from "Why did this happen?" to "What can I learn from it?"

Or take Elizabeth Smart, kidnapped at age 14 and subjected to unthinkable abuse. Years later, she forgave her captors in a public ceremony, not because they were worthy, but because she was tired of letting them control her life anymore. Her story teaches that forgiveness is not condoning. It's taking back your power.

When we forgive ourselves, we create room for growth. Guilt becomes guidance; regret turns into wisdom. The past loses its razor-sharp edges, and what's left behind is experience, raw, rich, and wonderfully human.

The Intention Behind Forgiveness

The words "Religion is intention and intention is religion" ring true across religions. So, too, with forgiveness: it is not about external action but internal intention. You can say "I forgive you," but unless your heart no longer grieves, the healing has not started.

All religious traditions underscore this inward aspect:

- In Christianity, Jesus uttered on the cross, "Father, forgive them, for they know not what they do." The action was not to eliminate injustice but to go beyond it by love.

- In Buddhism, the process of metta bhavana (loving-kindness meditation) conditions the heart to wish others good, even to those who have harmed others.

- For Islam, forgiveness (maghfirah) is one of the most underscored characteristics of Allah. According to the Qur'an, "Let them pardon and overlook. Would you not love for Allah to forgive you?"

- For Hinduism, the Mahabharata instructs that forgiveness is the attribute of the strong one. Yudhishthira's self-control, though wronged, represented spiritual maturity.

Through these religions, there is one strand that holds strong: sincerity of intention. You cannot pretend to be forgiving. You can only develop into it. Stories of Change Forgiveness not only heals the forgiver; it changes whole lives. Take the case of Immaculée Ilibagiza, one of the iconic examples of forgiveness, is a survivor of the Rwandan genocide.

She took refuge in a tiny bathroom with seven other women for 91 days while her family was killed. Years after, when she encountered the person who murdered her mother and brother, she said, "I forgive you." When questioned on how she could do this, she said, "Forgiveness is all I have left to give." Her story has motivated millions because it shows forgiveness not as a moral obligation but as an act of deep spiritual bravery. Or Malala Yousafzai, who was attacked by the Taliban for attending school. When she survived, she didn't go on a vengeful rampage; rather, she engaged in advocacy. "I do not hate the Taliban who shot me," she said.

"Even if there were a gun in my hand and he was standing in front of me, I would not shoot him." Malala's forgiveness wasn't based on denial; it was based on strength.

It transformed her agony into a worldwide movement of education and peace.
Then there's Viktor Frankl, psychiatrist and Holocaust survivor, author of Man's Search for Meaning. "Everything can be taken from a man but one thing: the last of the human freedoms, to choose one's attitude." Frankl's forgiveness was not of people but of life itself. He chose not to allow hate to shape his soul. His pain taught him the most.

Practical Ways to Heal Through Forgiveness

Acknowledge the Hurt.

Healing starts with naming the wound. Write down what occurred, how it affected you, and what you lost. No judgment, just note.

See the Person Behind the Pain.
Do your best to see your abuser as a human. People behave out of their own brokenness. Knowing this does not excuse them, but it allows you to let go emotionally.

Shift the Story.
Rather than saying over and over again, "I was betrayed," try shifting to, "I learned whom to trust." Replace victimhood with awareness.

Practice Gratitude.
Gratitude can feel far away from forgiveness, but it's closely linked. When you concentrate on what is still good, your mind starts softening.

Meditate on Compassion.
Picture extending kindness to those who harmed you. This isn't about liking them; it's about releasing yourself from the toxin of hate.

Forgive Gradually.
Forgiveness doesn't necessarily come overnight. You may forgive in layers, first with your head, then your heart, and finally your soul. Let the process develop naturally.

The Forgiveness Science

Contemporary psychology concurs with what ancient wisdom has known for ages: holding a grudge is not only hurting your spirit but also your body. Researchers at Stanford University found that forgiveness lowers blood pressure, promotes better heart health, and improves sleep. Neuroscientists claim it reprograms the brain by soothing the amygdala (fear center) and engaging areas associated with empathy.

When you forgive, you literally transform your biology. You switch from survival mode to growth mode. You're no longer responding to the past; you're building your future.

The Freedom Beyond

Forgiveness isn't about saying, "It's okay." It's about saying, "I'm okay." It's claiming that your peace doesn't rest on anyone else's apology. When you forgive, you reclaim your energy for yourself.

As mentioned earlier, all those people rose above testifying that strength is not in fighting back, but in rising above. Their forgiveness was a legacy, not a concession.

Forgiveness does not erase your story; it distills it. It doesn't make you forget; it allows you to remember differently. Every scar maps out the path of growth; every tear marks the sign of release.

So, if you catch yourself hanging on to an old wound, ask: What is this pain still trying to teach me? Sometimes the lesson isn't about justice, it's about peace. Sometimes, forgiveness isn't a gift to someone else; it's a holy return to yourself.

Because at the end of every spiritual path, every faith, and every broken heart, one thing holds true: To forgive is to release a prisoner from jail, and then find that the prisoner was you.

Chapter 13 – The Power of Reflection

There is a time, usually in private isolation, that you stop and reflect on your path and see that all of the decisions, the falls, and the rises have led you to the person you are today. Remembering is not reflection; it's comprehension. It is the practice of stopping to have an opportunity to see oneself. Not this one people see, but this one you may see behind your eyes- the thinker, the dreamer, the struggling, the believing.

When you have traversed the previous chapters, you have already passed through thoughts that are eternal and very human at the same time, which are attitude, ego, faith, integrity, forgiveness, and purpose. They are not the abstract virtues; they are the invisible threads that hold our lives together. But reflection is what ties them into meaning. Without reflection, wisdom remains scattered. With it, life becomes a narrative, coherent, purposeful, alive.

Let's revisit these lessons, not as moral advice checkboxes, but as guiding stars for the future.

The Mirror of Attitude: Seeing Possibility in Everything

We started with attitude, that quiet filter through which we view the world. You were told that things do not always go in a planned, but how you respond to what happens is the key to becoming a victim or a victor. Positive attitude does not mean denial, bounce-back-ability. Consider the case of Thomas Edison, who did not succeed in thousands of attempts to invent the light bulb. He was asked what his failures were, and he replied that he had not failed. I have just discovered 10,000 ways that will not work.

That is the magic of thinking at the moment. Rather than condemning his mistakes, he redefined them. Reflection provides you with the same power to redefine struggle as strength. Every time you take a moment to ask yourself, "What is this teaching me?", you turn a problem into a teacher.

The Invisible Wall of Ego: Learning to Step Aside

Then ego arrived, the unseen barrier that twists perception. Ego informs you that you are always correct, that your value hinges on comparison. It thrives on insecurity and starves your capacity to connect. The antidote? Self-awareness.

According to Mahatma Gandhi, who once said: The best way to discover yourself is to lose yourself in the service of other people. You begin to make a difference between confidence and arrogance, between self-respect and pride when you take a look back at what you were thinking. Reflection helps in making ego tender, as you have the realization that progress only takes place when you are humble enough to realize that you have so much to learn.

Overconfidence: The Sweet Trap

In the following chapter, we discussed overconfidence, the delusion that you've arrived when you've only just started. History is replete with examples: businesses that dismissed innovation, leaders who underestimated difficulty, and individuals who confused momentum with mastery. Self-reflection shields you from that trap.

Self-reflection poses the questions, "Am I listening enough?" and "Am I learning from those who dissent?" It's humility in action. Real self-confidence doesn't yell, it listens. It adapts.

Faith Beyond Boundaries

When we wrote of spiritual lessons across religions, the message was brief but deep: doing good is universal. Whether it's Christianity's "Love thy neighbor," Islam's "To save one life is as if to save all of humanity," Hinduism's "Vasudhaiva Kutumbakam" (the world is one family), or Buddhism's loving-kindness towards all beings, the message is the same.

Reflection makes this reality stick. It challenges you to wonder, "Am I living according to the values I respect?" Faith isn't belief, it's practice. It's the daily decision to be generous when no one will see, to forgive when pride says otherwise, to serve when it's inconvenient.

Purpose Over Applause

The chapter "Live for a Cause, Not for Applause" reminded you that life's deepest satisfaction doesn't come from approval but from giving. Reflection grounds you in purpose. When you stop to ask, "Why am I doing this?", you get back in line with significance.

Mother Teresa, serving in quiet for decades before anyone even knew her name. Or Greta Thunberg, starting a one-woman protest that inspired a worldwide climate movement. They didn't do it for accolades; they did it out of belief. That's what it means to live for a purpose.

When you consider your motivations, you see that completion is inward, not outward. Applause wanes, but intent resonates.

Integrity in the Face of Hardship

You will be tested on your ethics in life. You always are. In "Integrity in the Face of Hardship," you learned that honesty is not about being convenient; it's about character. When everything hangs in the balance, integrity is your guide.

Every time you take a stand for integrity, you reinforce your inner core. And at some point, you'll sit back and notice that while the world itself turned upside down, your inner core remained unscathed.

Ethics in Money and Business: Clean Hands, Clear Mind

We inhabit a universe that is fixated on results, profits, power, and progress. But what then about the process? The chapter "Ethics in Business and Money" learned that achievement without ethics is a fleeting win. Reflection is your insurance policy against the allure of shortcuts.

Money earned with integrity weighs less; it has no guilt attached, no fear. Self-reflection keeps you grounded in that honesty.

No Shortcuts: The Road That Tests You

Hard work is not glamorous, but it's holy. In "No Shortcuts on the Road to Success," we learned that effort creates character in ways that shortcuts or luck never could. The pandemic years taught the world that perseverance and flexibility are more valuable than sheer ambition.

When you do fail, and you will, reflection keeps despair at bay. It tells you that failure is not an endpoint but a detour. Every failure is a checkpoint that queries, "Are you on course with your purpose?" Each reflection makes you stronger.

Belief in Yourself: The Voice Within

"Never Underestimate Yourself" was all about taking back faith. Doubt is a robber; it takes away chances before you even get the chance to attempt them. Reflection makes you aware that the person saying "you can't" isn't reality, it's fear.

Eleanor Roosevelt once quoted, "No one can make you feel inferior without your consent." You look at how far you've come, how much courage you've exhibited, and how many storms you've weathered when you look back on your path.

Self-confidence isn't arrogance, it's self-consciousness. It's acknowledging your flaws and yet having the courage to say, "Yes, I can."

Forgiveness: The Ultimate Freedom

The section "Forgiveness and the Intention to Heal" reminded you that healing starts with release. Forgiveness is not about them, it's about you. It's about taking back your energy from hurt.

Reflection is the vehicle that allows forgiveness to happen. If you sit still and go back to those times that pained you, something magical occurs: perspective. You start realizing that the ones who caused you pain were broken as well, that the hurt was part of your development, and that you don't have to carry what doesn't serve you anymore.

Forgiveness is a reflection made flesh. It's the heart proclaiming, "I release you. I free me."

Why Reflection Is the Key to Everything

Reflection is not thinking; it's living consciously. It's stopping to check if your direction aligns with your destination. It's the dialogue you share with your soul.

There's a tradition in Japanese philosophy called Naikan, which literally means "looking inside." It's asking yourself three questions every evening:

What have I received today?

What did I give today?

What did I trouble today?

Think about doing that every day. How much more conscious, compassionate, and thankful you'd become.

Reflection isn't regret, it's realignment. Daily reflection means you stop reacting and begin to respond. You stop drifting and begin to direct. You become the writer of your own script.

Writing Your Own Ladder of Success

Everyone's ladder appears differently. Success to one may be stability. To another, it is creativity or contribution. Self-reflection allows you to determine what success is to you, not what society says it should be.

Create your own ladder. Every rung is a value, not an achievement: honesty, empathy, curiosity, gratitude, persistence. Every time you live them, you climb. You may go up slower than others, but you will never fall. Because your ladder is made of truth.

Take a moment and ask yourself:

- What does success mean to me?
- What do I want to become as I get there?
- If I lost everything external, money, fame, titles, would I still respect myself?

These questions don't have one-time answers; they're meant to evolve with you.

A Personal Letter to You

If you've come this far, thank you for reading, for reflecting, and for believing that change begins with awareness. Writing this book was not an act of teaching; it was an act of sharing. Every chapter was born from observation, from the belief that humanity, despite its chaos, is still capable of kindness, courage, and consciousness.

If just one percent of you improves, just one slight adjustment in attitude, one act of compassion, one decision of character, this book has won out.

Because revolution doesn't start with change. It starts with introspection.

Carve out ten minutes a day. Sit in silence. Breathe profoundly. Ask yourself, "Did I live today on purpose?" That's it. And over time, those minutes will form your thoughts, your relationships, and the path of your life.

You hold the pen to your story. Reflection is the ink. Your life, your choices, your words, and your acts of goodness are the masterpiece waiting to be written.

So, pause. Reflect. And begin again, with purpose, with peace, and with the unshakable belief that the best chapters of your life are the ones you've yet to write.

Verses Kindler Publication

Verses Kindler Publication

Verses Kindler Publication

Reach us through our website -
https://www.verseskindlerpublication.com/
For more information visit our
Instagram or Facebook page.

Connect with the author at –
Intentionbykhuzema.com
khuzemakhan@gmail.com

9 789347 494673

Printed at Repro India Ltd.